HELPING YOURSELF
WITH
WHITE WITCHCRAFT

Also by the Same Author

Helping Yourself with ESP
Helping Yourself with Psycho-Cosmic Power

HELPING YOURSELF
WITH
WHITE WITCHCRAFT

Al G. Manning, B.S., D.D.

Parker Publishing Company, Inc.   *West Nyack, N.Y.*

Dedication

Dedicated to the reader of this book.
May it help you achieve your goals
and desires.

© 1972, by
Parker Publishing Company, Inc.
West Nyack, N.Y.

20

Library of Congress Cataloging in Publication Data

Manning, Al G
    Helping yourself with white witchcraft.

    1. Witchcraft. 2. Success. I. Title.
BF1566.M277   131'.32   72-8115
ISBN 0-13-386565-7

Printed in the United States of America

What This Book Can Do for You

*A*re you *master of your own destiny?* Would you like to be? For each of us there are times of uncertainty and seemingly insurmountable problems. When they come, are you fully equipped to handle them? Or could you use some truly powerful, help? The arcane forces of White Witchcraft can provide such a power for you! Hidden within the ancient lore of the religion, Wicca (now called White Witchcraft), is a power sufficient to meet your *every* need. The traditional rituals and practices of the White Witch attract a literally invincible power and subject it to *your* control. You can serve yourself well by learning how to do it.

What White Witchcraft Is

White Witchcraft is a combination of magical practices including ritual use of herbs, oils, candles, incense and the power of constructive will to attract and harness the occult forces of the universe for the benefit of an individual or group of individuals. We distinguish White Witchcraft from the "Black Arts" by the intent to produce benefits and *not* harm. There is no need to harm another being—by using the great powers of White Witchcraft, you will quickly find that there is plenty of good to go around. You need take from no other person, simply build your own good fortune and happiness out of the universal energies which are available in abundance to everyone.

What White Witchcraft Can Do for You

The Ceremonial Magic of White Witchcraft can harness tremendous occult power to bring you *personal* benefits of any kind.

Invisible, but very real forces will protect you from harm and open the doors of success to your every goal—when you order them ceremonially as a White Witch. As you assume this great power, you will not look different from your neighbors, except for the special brightness and air of confidence that naturally comes with success.

The years of research and practical experimentation behind this book proved that firm understanding of the forces you will be using brings power that far surpasses anything generated by blind faith. Thus there are no strange sounds or syllables to add confusion to your rituals—everything is given in simple English with the certain knowledge that *you* can generate the power because *you know what you are doing.* Our approach is simple, step by step mastery of the amazing powers of Witchcraft, that you may fulfill your purpose in life by realizing that you are indeed the master of your destiny. There are rewards for each step that you master, and I assure you you will enjoy the work. Nothing adds zest to your activities like success piled upon happy success!

White Witchcraft works for people just like you! On Page 88 you will find the story of how Irene R. used the love ritual and wound up happily married to her former boss. Page 102 tells you how B.J. used the Money/Prosperity Attracting Ritual to borrow $250,000 for his company that had a $50,000 negative net worth, and later sell the company for over a million dollars. Page 197 shows you how S.Y. followed the advice of a self-induced prophetic dream and saved $300,000! And there are plenty more examples from happily successful people in all walks of life. Many of the people who have participated in our Witchcraft programs, are prominent business executives and scientists. Invariably, the highly successful ones have asked us to use fictitious names or generalize the circumstances enough to protect their privacy and professional reputations. Wouldn't you? Our typical report begins, "Please *don't* use my name with this true story. But this is what happened. . . ."

Within the limits of individual privacy, the reports of success with the White Witchcraft rituals given in this book are in our files at our E.S.P. Laboratory. I am looking forward to adding *your* reports of success gained through White Witchcraft.

THIS BOOK IS MEANT TO BE USED IN YOUR DAILY LIVING—
TO YOUR PRACTICAL BENEFIT

There is no "patter" or academic history in this book. Every word is intended to be useful to you in the most practical sense. But it will remain just an accumulation of words on paper until *you* put it into practice. Give this effective system of using primitive and occult power a full opportunity to upgrade every part of your life the way you want it to.

The powerful truths of ancient rituals, reproduced in modern words, are waiting within the pages of this book—they are waiting to serve *you*. And because they are part of the Law of the Universe, they cannot refuse to serve you!

But be careful how you share your knowledge. When the Witchcraft rituals work for you because you put your whole being into them, they are true for you—and it is not important whether anyone else believes. In fact it may be more comfortable for you if others simply don't know how successfully you have applied White Witchcraft to your life.

The best course for you and the world is not to flaunt or ridicule, but simply use the great and satisfying power which this book is ready to bring you. *Your* success, growth, power, and fulfillment are the good reasons for this book. Don't waste them! Learn and *do,* and walk confidently along your path of success in everything through White Witchcraft.

Al G. Manning

CONTENTS

Chapter One

How to Organize Yourself
for Effective Uses of
White Witchcraft

Charlie, Jack and Larry were equally qualified for the leadman position. Charlie got the job, but he didn't keep it long—he was quickly promoted to foreman! Why? And how did plain little Mary marry the local millionaire? The answer to these and many similar questions can be found in the modern day practice of Witchcraft. If the normal things are equal and *you* are not practicing Witchcraft, then you're the loser! Why not become a happy winner? You will find it richly rewarding to investigate the practical aspects of Ceremonial Magic or shall we call it White Witchcraft? Let's take a good look at the fundamentals of Witchcraft and how to organize them for your benefit.

WITCHCRAFT AND HOW IT CAN HELP YOU

What is Witchcraft, and what is a White Witch? White Witchcraft is the method, and its practitioner is a White Witch. The actual process is the harnessing of the unseen, but very real, forces that control the universe—and bending them to control it in *your* favor. We distinguish a White Witch from a practitioner of the "Black Arts" by understanding that a White Witch is careful never to harm another being. And the reason is simple, you are too busy reaping your own good fortune to be the least bit interested in disturbing the good of someone else.

The ancient religion of Wicca (Wicca is the root of the word Witchcraft) is intensely practical! It's origin can be traced to man's need to attune with the Nature Spirits to insure good crops and good hunting. Some of the old fertility rites have been perverted to devil worship by a few publicity seekers, but there is a vast storehouse of power in the beautiful and pure ancient ceremonies that should not be discarded because of a few negative people. The modern Witch works with natural *energy*—and we can certainly agree that *all energy is potentially good*. Electricity is an excellent example. We can use it to light a city or kill a man in the "electric chair"—the energy itself is neutral, but man uses it for his own purposes which may or may not be "good." Here your own conscience must be your guide. But the *power is available to you*, and it would be foolish to ignore it.

Matters of love, prosperity, personal power, security, protection, health and "good luck" are the natural field for the application of your powers of Witchcraft. Possibly *you* were a practicing Witch in one of your past lives! So why not regain your old powers and add some new ones to make them more effective for practical use now. You can definitely enrich your own life, and the lives of others as well.

The principles and rituals presented in this book are not based on speculation or simply gleaned from laboriously pouring through musty manuscripts. The research was not limited to books and papers, but included detail regressions to past lives of many people. What we learned was presented in class work at my E.S.P. Laboratory in Los Angeles and tested under real life conditions by a wide cross section of normal, respectable human beings. We threw away the chaff and happily present here the part *that works!* The real proof comes not from the examples we will give, but from the *results* as *it works for you!*

One of our highly successful students told how her interest in White Witchcraft was whetted: "I thought this was a bunch of nonsense until I went to work in a big restaurant. Whenever business slowed down, the Chef would walk out to us carrying a salt and herb mixture. He'd say, 'I'll get them coming in again!' And take a quick walk around the building sprinkling his mixture. It invariably worked. Within ten minutes after he sprinkled his witch mixture, the place would be full of people. I decided I'd like to know more about the power he harnessed so easily!"

Love, money, power, beauty, security—all are within your reach as you apply the principles that will be unfolded to you in this book. But let's keep a good measure of common sense along with it. Don't be like the student who called me up to complain that he hadn't won the lottery he had used a ritual for. I asked him what day he bought his ticket and the astonished reply was, "I didn't realize I had to actually buy a ticket to win!" Ritual, herbs, oils, incenses and powders are powerful indeed, but they need the help of common sense and good old-fashioned dedicated work at the "right time." Now let's set up the important first steps for your success in using White Witchcraft.

THE WITCH'S PYRAMID AND HOW YOU BUILD IT

Witchcraft is primarily a state or attitude of mind. The traditional pointed witch's hat is symbolic of a power yet hidden in the Great Pyramid—at least as far as modern science is concerned. We will touch this power in many ways throughout this book. I hinted at much that will come here in my book, *Helping Yourself with Psycho-Cosmic Power,* Parker Publishing Co., West Nyack, N.Y., but it took six more years of research to make us ready to bring the many principles together in the name of White Witchcraft. The term *Witch* applies to *either* sex, and we should distinguish ourselves from the lesser terms applied to males such as "wizard" or "warlock."

To begin our work say aloud, "I am a Witch! I am a happy, successful White Witch, and I intend to enjoy life more and more each day!" A Witch is also an eclectic—we must borrow our knowledge and power from any and all systems that work, and then make them work better for us. Let's begin with the allegorical Witch's Pyramid. This might be called a mental model of the Great Pyramid, but it is *your* most important tool. The base of your pyramid is a square having for its four corners (1) Constructive Will (2) Creative Imagination (3) Faith, and (4) Secrecy. When the four corners are balanced and functioning, they emit the energy that adds the top point of the pyramid, Accomplishment.

In the book, *Helping Yourself with Psycho-Cosmic Power,* I gave a simplified version of the Witch's Pyramid which I called the basic Formula for Creation. In *Psycho-Cosmic Power* the formula seemed easier, but in our Witchcraft we expect the results to be more reliable because we are bringing more power into it. As we used the formula in *Psycho-Cosmic Power* it was: "The idea, held in conscious imagination and reinforced by sound, calls forth the energy of creation." That's all there was to it. And by the way, it works! Don't let anybody tell you it doesn't. When you contemplate an idea long enough and generate positive enthusiasm about it—it will manifest! In the arts of White Witchcraft, we make the process more complicated and add the effectiveness of ritual, but we're doing much the same thing. We will add extra tools of visualization, ritual, constructive will and cooperative nature spirits to keep all the energy focused in one place and gain your manifestation or realize your goals more certainly. So, for this work in White Witchcraft we will expand our thinking to a four-step formula for creation as follows:

THE FOUR STEPS OF CREATION BY WHITE WITCHCRAFT

1) Desire fires the *creative imagination* and in combination with ritual generates the emotion—enthusiam.

2) The emotional energy of enthusiasm is ritually controlled and shaped by your power of *constructive will*. Constructive will acts to mould the energy instead of letting it fly off in all directions to be wasted. This moulding of the energy is the actual creation of a living being that we will call a *thoughtform.*

3) The *thoughtform* is nurtured by *faith* and fed with regular doses of enthusiasm and love.

4) Your living *thoughtform* entity is protected by *secrecy,* until it manifests.

You will note that this formula uses the four points of the base of your Witch's Pyramid. As we go through the work, we will illustrate this in many ways. But let's give careful consideration to interference. Just as in metaphysics, doubt will block your manifestation—thus the call for secrecy. It's true that part of being a good Witch may include the innuendo and mystique that adds to the illusion of your power among your associates. But secrecy is equally important—never expose a tender growing *thoughtform* to the ridicule or doubt of another. This would not only kill the development of a particular project but also weaken the very structure of your Power Pyramid.

Central to the whole operation is that most often missing ingredient, Constructive Will. Before you can function with any degree of effectiveness, this tool must be developed.

How to Generate the Full Power of Constructive Will

Just as a truly great musician practices the scales daily, so you, if you would be an effective Witch, must practice a few fundamentals daily. In this beginning stage we will give you several exercises for "homework." We suggest that you concentrate on each exercise for a full week, but then don't forget it. Warm up for your Witchcraft work with the power exercises even as the musician will warm up by playing the scales. <u>Power is a direct result of discipline</u>. *You can be infinitely powerful!* Let's set about building the disciplines that make it so.

We seek first to build your discipline of constructive Will. Let's not be confused with what the average person calls "will power." The normal meaning of "will power" is really "won't power," such as: "I won't eat that extra piece of cake," or "I won't smoke anymore." "Won't power" presupposes an adversary and a struggle, thus for all but the Spartan few it is quite a waste of effort—producing nothing but a feeling of frustration and a failure consciousness. In effective Witchcraft, we put the emphasis on the opposite—*"I Will"!*

Begin by telling yourself, "<u>*I will* be positive</u>. *I will* be a force so strong that all the things which used to sap away my power are rendered completely ineffective. Then set out to prove it to yourself. <u>*Exercise your constructive will power*</u> for the week to come. <u>Make a list of seven things you have been avoiding or "putting off" for the work of this most important week of your life</u>. *This is your week to become a winner!* <u>Each day of this one week, you are to tackle one of the items on your list, *face it* and win!*</u> We're going to build the confidence and consciousness of a winner by deciding about each day's personal assignment: "Come hell or high water, I'm going to *do it!* I'll find the time or make the time if I have to stay up all night."

Make the list as easy as you need to feel comfortable, but make it and *win!* The little challenges will come along—your resolve will be tested by circumstances. But this is not a test of won't power, it is an exercise of *positive accomplishment*. We can never fully stress the personal growth potential of repeating this exercise one week out of every month. The *habit of winning* is what we seek. Here's a sample list of the seven day constructive will exercise for Mary S., a highly successful new Witch:

Sunday: Clean out the hall closet (It's been a mess for years, but no more!)
Monday: Write that long overdue letter to Aunt Margaret.

Tuesday: Clean out the "junk drawer" in my office desk.

Wednesday: Get to that pile of messy work I've been putting off at the office.

Thursday: Straighten out my file cabinet at the office.

Friday: Clean the bedroom curtains and windows.

Saturday: Spend 2 hours reviewing *Helping Yourself with Psycho-Cosmic Power.*

Cleaning out the closet proved to be fun and turned up a couple of useful lost items—one was a cute pin she wore to work on Monday for a reminder. Monday brought the first challenge to her resolve. Just as Mary got home from work, the phone rang with an invitation to an impromptu party. She accepted, but promised herself to write the letter when she returned. It was a bit late, but the extra 20 minutes spent in letter writing brought more accomplishment than the time in bed was worth—and she slept with a smile of satisfaction on her face. Tuesday it took part of her lunch hour to clean out that junk drawer, but again there was a reward of a long forgotten keepsake that brought special satisfaction. Wednesday's office work load was a big challenge, but somehow she managed to whittle down that "mess" pile. By quitting time it was gone—and Mary had a whole new handle on life. The joy of winning built a new constructive will that has changed her forever. No wonder she is such a successful Witch!

Long Range Projects

Long range projects are excellent for building this most useful discipline of constructive will. Do you want to write a book? Would you like a six-month vacation to do it? I'll bet you it wouldn't work that way! All my books have been written as exercises in constructive will. It's a game! You must write at least two pages of manuscript each day. During a creative burst, you may get ahead, but under *no* circumstances may you go to bed on Sunday night without the fourteen pages for the week completed. Rewrites go faster, you can set a three or perhaps four page a day goal. But sickness, family disaster, fire, flood, earthquake or a good time are not excuses—there is only one way to win—by *doing!* The term "drive" comes closer to explaining constructive will than any of normal man's concepts, but a good witch will make it mean much more.

HOW TO ENHANCE YOUR CREATIVE IMAGINATION

The powerful tool of creative imagination comes from breaking the bonds of "in a rut" thinking. The Satanist Cults would have you begin by reciting the Lord's Prayer backwards as a symbol of being your "own man," but I prefer to keep on good terms with early religious training and use its strong points to reinforce our positive ritual work—if we are to be good eclectics, we must accept the good and useful parts of all religions with the positive White Witch attitude of not tearing down, but always building!

Free Thinking

Free thinking certainly is necessary. We have been carefully programmed by the world to accept a bunch of inhibitions and taboos some of which are utterly ridiculous. I was raised in the "Hard-shell Baptist" country long enough ago that I trust I'm not stepping any toes to tell this story. I was a little fellow about seven and had learned to crochet hooked rugs. One Sunday morning I was sitting on my bed working on a rug when my dear great aunt caught me. She started to rant and rave, "My heavens, you're crocheting on Sunday! You'll have to pull out every stitch with your nose *in hell,* boy!" You may laugh but there is some of this old "fire and brimstone" shackle lurking around every one of us. This is one of many examples of stereotyped thinking that we must break if we are to own the tool of creative imagination. We will approach this work with two exercises—give yourself the benefit of a full week on each.

Exercise to Develop Your Creative Imagination

1st Week: Select a different simple household object each day for the seven days of this exercise. Examples would be a pencil, spoon, cup, knife, fork, bottle, ruler, book, toothpaste tube, etc. Spend 15 minutes each night observing your selected object in detail and mystically attuning with it—be able to reproduce it in mental picture form, but also to list 50 to 100 different uses for it. That's where your imagination comes in! Anybody can think of stirring with a spoon, but how about propping open a window, a pole for a homemade battery, part of a piece of modern sculpture, or add many of your own!

There are lots of benefits from this week's exercise. Most psychology books touch on the classic story of taking the subject into a nearly empty room. He is told that there is a ping pong ball down in the rusty old pipe standing in one corner of the room. His assignment is to get it out. In another corner of the room is a lovely table set with sterling silver, crystal and a pitcher of water. In the middle of the room is a wooden stick, a screw driver and a set of wrenches. Of course none of the tools work and ninety-nine subjects out of a hundred flunk—they never think to pour the water from the beautiful pitcher into the rusty pipe to float the ping pong ball to the top. The beauty of the table setting just doesn't connect with the rusty pipe. Too often our routine world gets us locked into narrow thought patterns that restrict our creativity. Use this exercise to deliberately break free from the old inhibitions and limiting sterotypes lurking in the dark recesses of your mind.

2nd Week: Expand last week's idea of exercising your imagination by finding new ways of doing your routine things. Never go to work the same way twice (at least for this one week). And start looking for your limiting hang-ups. It's amazing how much worn out routine we drag along from the past. Try to find a new and more effective way to do every routine task—turn loose and imagine fantastic schemes, then let them scale themselves down to practical usefulness. The idea is to let your imagination go free, but under control so you might call it a controlled daydream. How free a thinker are you? Would it bother you to have me say that I do all my serious ritual work clad only in an ankh necklace? What shocks you? Is it real or something that was pounded into your head when you were six years old? Our aim is to challenge all your inhibitions—not necessarily to change a single outward act, but to change the *why* you do them. How long has it been since you had a wild idea and didn't talk yourself back out of it? This is the week to build fresh spontaneity into all areas of your life.

How Jerry S. Used Free Thinking to Get a Promotion

Jerry S., a young assistant personnel manager challenged the usefulness of a major departmental publication during this exercise. His spontaneity proved so convincing that the revision saved his company $600 per month. He just got a pat on the back for that one, but after several more ideas that improved departmental efficiency came the promotion and the nice raise. Honest effort on the first few weekly exercises will bring wonders to your life all by themselves, but they will also build the power and discipline necessary to truly effective witchcraft. Let's look now at some of the physical witch tools.

Your Witch's Working Tools

Spellbook (or Grimoire): When you have a highly successful demonstration of your witch power, you will certainly want to remember exactly how you did it so you can do it again should the occasion demand. A good quality loose-leaf notebook is best, so you can occasionally clean out the accumulation of not so effective spells. This should be planned as a combination diary and recipe book. It is very personal, and the necessity for secrecy is obvious, you'll find that a degree of reverence in handling it will pay dividends. Establish this rewarding practice from the very beginning of your work: record date, time and the details of each ritual performed or spell cast. In a few months you'll find you have a priceless record of your growth and proficiency. And should you encounter the term, *Grimoire*, in your research, you'll know that the writer was speaking about a witch's secret recipe book.

Altar: The householder's altar of Buddhism could be an interesting parallel to the altar of Witchcraft. A small table makes an ideal altar, but just as in Buddhism it could be a tray that you put away after each ceremony. The minimum requirements for your altar would be two candle holders (the style should suit your individual taste), an incense burner, 2 small cups (one each of water and earth) and of course a candle snuffer—no self-respecting witch would ever blow out a candle! A mirror will prove very useful in advanced ritual work also.

Chalice, Mortar and Pestle, Chafing Dish: When we begin mixing your potions and witch's brews you'll need a large cup or chalice and a chafing dish (or some suitable container that can hold burning charcoal without setting fire to the place). And unless you are careful to acquire only finely powdered herbs, a simple mortar and pestle such as you will find in any hobby shop is virtually indispensable.

Cord and Knife (or Athame´): Your witch's cord can be worn as a sash or belt—it is also used as a drawing compass to lay out the nine and seven foot ritual circles. Your cord should be made with your own hands by braiding together six strips of bright red ribbon. It should be knotted at the 3 1/2 foot mark and at the 4 1/2 foot mark to indicate the radius of the traditional circles. (Its length: 4 1/2 to 6 feet.) The knife or Athame´ should have a blade six to eight inches long and a plain handle on which you will inscribe your witch's name and other symbology later. This is used for drawing the symbolic circle and many other interesting parts of your rituals.

The Hat, Robes and Other Apparel (or Lack Thereof): Let me begin by commenting that the best of all Witch costumes is the lovely suit of skin in which you entered this world. For some coven (means place) work (or on an extremely cold night) one might resort to simple robes, but the physical and psychological freedom expressed by the absence of clothing fits beautifully into the ancient traditions of fertility and oneness with nature that are the great power of true Witchcraft. My favorite exception would be the pointed hat—note the similarity to the "dunce cap" and the pyramid. There is a powerful energy in the properly constructed pyramid and we can understand the cone as simply a pyramid with an infinite number of sides. A stiff paper is easiest for this purpose and if you're impelled in this direction try a diameter of seven inches for the bottom and let the altitude of the hat be just under five inches. We will come back to Pyramid Power in a later chapter.

My idea in presenting this here is that you can be on the lookout for suitable items while you study and digest the details of a spell-casting and ritual work presented as we progress.

THE IMPORTANCE OF RITUAL—OR
HOW TO HARNESS THE POWER OF HABIT

It's amazing how completely we are creatures of habit. Our good habits carry us through the toughest of situations and keep us in balance, while the "bad" ones prove the strength of this power. Those who have tried unsuccessfully to stop smoking are living testimony to habit's ability to control human behavior. But why do we talk of habit in connection with ritual? Simply because ritual creates habit. Consider the ritual of getting up on a workday morning. Are you sure you could vary it? You struggle up and stagger to the shower or to brush your teeth, and it's mostly instinctive. I've known people who didn't start to function under full conscious control until they were "up" for five or six hours. Haven't you? Or are you one?

Just as a good morning ritual will get you to work on time, so a good Witchcraft ritual will build the power to accomplish your chosen goal. The first ritual should be our suggested homework of the first week—building the habit of *success*. Call it constructive will or a success consciousness, but put out the effort to get it and we'll parlay it into a genie to do your every bidding! But let's add a bit of balance right here. All ritual work requires the light touch to be effective. If you're too "dead pan" serious, you'll make it so flat that nothing happens. The harder you *try*, the more you lose the happy constructive will that we're working so hard to build. The real secret of all successful Witchcraft is to be so confident that you can relax. Nothing works so well as sheer confidence balanced by the little child's awe that's just slightly flip—"I'm not quite sure, but I'll sure enjoy trying!"

One of our students, Sarah N., reported on her first week of the constructive will exercise: "I decided to quit resenting my pay status and ask for a raise. Not only did I get the biggest raise ever given to a woman in the history of the company, but I was promised another in three months! This stuff works!" This happened on the fifth day of her ritual, she let the feeling of victory proceed her and it paid off—just as it will for you.

THE IMPORTANCE OF HELP FROM
INCENSE, OILS, HERBS AND POWDERS

A friend of mine rushed excitedly up to me exclaiming: "I just found a wonderfully way-out group! They light candles on a big altar, burn lots of incense, use prayer beads, wear fancy robes, and chant in a strange language. It's really far out!"

So I asked: "What is it"?

He answered with a twinkle in his eye, "The Orthodox Church."

Indeed the great strength of the organized Orthodox Church comes from the time when all of its rituals were alive and produced obvious spirit responses. The remnants of the rituals as practiced today still carry the natural power of odor and fire that attracts the elemental and nature spirits—as do certain herbs, powders and essences. As we go deeper into the work, we will discuss many of the herbs in detail and give time-tested formulae for potions and spells, some of which came forward all the way from the Witchcraft of the ancient continent called Atlantis. For now, let's simply suggest that you keep an open mind. The pragmatic test is the best—if it works, you will use it! But you can't tell if it works for you unless you *try*— with enthusiasm and sincerity in fairness to yourself.

CHAPTER POINTS TO REMEMBER

1) White Witchcraft is a religion of oneness with nature. It is beautiful and good when the energies are used constructively. Your neighbor may already be using these powers in secret. You owe it to yourself not to ignore the tangible benefits of strength and power that are readily available to you through the beautiful rituals and practices of Witchcraft.

2) The Witch's Pyramid is built of Constructive Will, Creative Imagination, Faith and Secrecy. The top of the pyramid is Accomplishment.

3) The four step formula for creation will work for you. It uses the four corners of your Witch's Pyramid. Use it to win victory after smashing victory.

4) Spend the full week on the exercise to build your constructive will. Then use it one week out of every month and enjoy a happy, effective life forevermore.

5) Use the two-week exercise to develop your creative imagination. This power will prove its value day after day after victorious day.

6) Begin gathering the simple tools of your new craft. The

Spellbook or Grimoire is your most important first tool. Begin yours immediately—even if you decide to copy it into a better book later.

7) We will prove the great value of ritual and the power of incense, oils and the like as this book unfolds *your* power.

Chapter Two

How to Cast Spells
in Witchcraft

*B*efore you begin your work to set the magical-psychic forces in action, it is important that you be completely protected. There is a tradition in Witchcraft that when a new student begins to work, he or she is to be tested as to sincerity and determination. Thus a nearby Witch or Demon who senses your initial efforts is apt to send a strong fear thought to literally frighten you away from your ritual. There is a real attempt to "separate the men from the boys," and lack of preparedness can rob you of your potentially great powers. Thus the beginning of all ritual work must be the setting of your protection against psychic attacks. Here then is a basic but powerful protective ritual. As you grow in understanding and proficiency, you will add and subtract to make the ritual truly your own. But for the first few weeks, *use this time tested method.*

Basic Protection Ritual

Your growing familiarity will add rich levels of understanding to each step of the ritual. In the beginning, some things may seem superfluous, but *don't omit any step*—at least until you are sure you understand the meaning and have accomplished the desired end in some other way.

Step 1. Tiling the Chamber: The first step is to set up physical and psychic safeguards. This is called "Tiling the Chamber." Physically you would lock the door (an ordinary screen door hook for your bedroom door is an easy way for instance) after taking your telephone off the hook (if it is in the room) and doing whatever else seems necessary to avoid interruption and insure your privacy.

For psychic protection one might anoint the body's orifices along with the brow and heart with a protective oil (Sandalwood will do in the beginning work), but the most important shield is an image of bright white light. Mentally build your protective light image all around and through the room and *know* that no creature of the darkness can enter the protective light.

Step 2. **Ritual Lighting of Candles and Incense:** Begin by sprinkling the area around your altar with a solution of salt in water from your cup or chalice. Put the cup with about half the liquid left on your altar beside the container of earth. Strike a match and use it to light the two candles, starting always with the candle on your right. White candles are best for protection. Yellow, blue or green will do nicely also, but *never* use a black candle—that would be an open invitation for the dark forces to take over your ceremony. Finally, light a protection incense (Sandalwood until you learn to choose your own) from the right-hand candle. Wave it around a bit to get the fragrant fumes spread nicely in the air before you place the burning incense in your incense burner. Then you are ready for a cleansing invocation.

Step 3. **Cleansing, Purification Invocation:** The 23rd, 46th or 91st Psalms in the Bible or all three could be used here, but I personally prefer to keep the ritual more completely nondenominational, so I call on the Vedantic Deity of Change, Lord Shiva, in the chant set forth below. Whether you use Psalms, the Shiva invocation or another prayer of your choice, it should be chanted aloud. Repeat the chanting until you *feel* a pleasant change in the atmosphere of the room.

INVOCATION OF SHIVA

Lovely, powerful Shiva, God of sweeping change,
  Sweep away the lesser, shut it out of range.
Leave the beauty and the Light bright and clean and fair,
  Remove all vibrations of misery and despair.
Leave this place and these fine things fresh and bright and pure,
  Holy as your own fine self, bright complete and sure.
Lovely, powerful Shiva, our thanks to you we give
  That from your sweeping power in beauty may we live.

Step 4. **Meditation upon Your worthiness:** More rituals produce zero or negative results than good ones for those who have haunting doubts about their personal worth. Now is the time to be sure that self doubt cannot rob you of your protection and personal power. Mentally or literally look at your reflection in the mirror (I use this literally, because an altar mirror is essential to my work), and say to it, "You're a very nice person. You are entitled to boundless success, happiness, riches and fulfillment." Then sit still and "listen" to the answer that comes back. All too often, the being in the mirror will object. It may seem to answer, "Oh, no you aren't"! But don't settle for that. Demand a specific answer, say, "Specifically, why not"? Then make notes of the "feedback" you get and resolve to do something about it!

If the task of gaining the approval of the face in your mirror is great, then stop your ritual and go to work on cleaning up the objectionable parts of your life. It would do you no good to continue anyway. The power we seek is absolutely omnipotent, but you cannot turn on the faucet until you get past that guardian of self. When you can get this far and the smiling face in the mirror agrees that you're a wonderful, deserving person, you're ready to begin the positive work.

Step 5. **Casting the Actual Spell:** Now hold up your hands with the palms facing a point on the middle of your altar. Visualize a stream of light shining from each hand and meeting at the point of power on your altar. *Feel* the power forming a living reality as you use the chant we will call Postulant's Invocation of Protection:

POSTULANT'S INVOCATION OF PROTECTION

> Spirit of the Great White Light,
>> Burn away my psychic night.
> Let me feel your loving care,
>> Give me joy and love to share.
> Make of me your willing tool,
>> Let fulfillment be the rule,
> That my growth may be a LIGHT,
>> Saving others from the night.

Repeat the chant nine times while you feel the power growing into a living entity right there on your altar. When you stop, reach out and "pet" the energy field that has gathered at your command at the altar—feel its power and know that it now has a life of its own, with its sole purpose to protect and care for *you.*

Step 6. **Closing the Ritual:** Even this elementary ritual may have attracted some elemental spirits who participated. So let's get used to dismissing the elementals. (We'll explain what they are and how they act in Chapter 4.) Say aloud in a firm voice: "To all elemental spirits gathered here, I thank you for your help and participation. Now go in peace back to your native habitats and harm no one on the way."

Next use a candle snuffer or your two fingers to extinguish the candle flames. A good witch or occultist would never blow out a candle—that would be a direct affront to the fire elementals as a symbol of dissipation of their energy. The snuffer gathers the flame into a small area that it may be symbolically preserved.

Finally close by thanking all your spirit help aloud: "I offer my thanks to the wonderful spirit beings who have participated and who are with me helping always."

Step 7. The Follow-Up: Like Rome, a good *thoughtform* spell is seldom built in one day. The ritual should be repeated each evening for one full week. Use this very simple ritual regularly as part of your development of Constructive Will. And because you are asking for help in cleaning up your life, many good things will be attracted to you.

How Cynthia S. Used the Ritual to Good Advantage

A young housewife, Cynthia S., felt that she and her husband were "stymied"—no future on his job, their two children were "always cranky and sick," and there was a running feud with the neighbors on both sides of them. She reported: "I waited for a full month to see if it was all just a lovely dream, but it is reality indeed! During the first week of using the Basic Protection Ritual, my husband got an unexpected promotion with a $100 a month raise, the kids suddenly became "dolls" and have stayed healthy, and both of my neighbors who had seemed so hostile invited me to coffee and have been most friendly and cooperative. The whole world could scream that this is coincidence, but it wouldn't convince me! I know that I'm on the right path to power and growth!"

Sam O's Case

Sam O. worked on the very busy order desk of an electronic supply firm. The pressure and confusion were difficult to cope with and he seemed constantly "on the carpet" for making too many mistakes. When Sam tried the basic protection ritual, it seemed natural to invite the protective *thoughtform* to "come on to work with me." From the very first day, the pressure seemed easier to handle and Sam's mistakes dwindled to almost nothing. Within a month the criticism from his boss had turned to praise and a $25 per month raise. Three more months brought Sam a promotion. His comment is: "I use my ritual every morning and I intend to keep it up for the rest of my life. Progress and success are too precious to be neglected."

THE IMPORTANCE OF EXORCISM

There are two basic definitions of *exorcism*. The first is to *bind by oath,* the second is to rid a *person or place of evil spirits.* In this early section of the book we will emphasize the *bind by oath* part as a way of gaining the cooperation of the nature spirits and "Little People" (psychic entities or beings). This use of the term, exorcism, might also be called a process of *consecration*. So, to distinguish this from the later work of chasing away "evil spirits," we will refer to this form of exorcism as *consecration*.

The purpose of this section is to give you the benefit of years of research and regression work undertaken for the specific purpose of learning how to get practical, tangible help from mystic or metaphysical sources in handling the every day affairs of our life. We found ritual most effective in harnessing the natural forces represented by the *elemental spirits* and *nature spirits* (or little people). Elaborate rituals have value in generating energy patterns to mightily reinforce existing habits or help bend them to more useful forms. Since the natural forces are at work all the time, we can gain much help by bending their habits to help us rather than act at random as they otherwise would.

This basic altar consecration ceremony is designed to put your ritual work in tune with nature's happily powerful forces. For all our work you will need to have your altar set up with at least two candle holders (white candles are best unless you're working for a specific purpose as we will discuss in a later chapter) an incense burner, a chalice (an ordinary coffee mug will do at first), incense (Sandlewood is excellent unless you have a favorite protective incense already), exorcism oil (again Sandalwood will do, but I prefer a mixture of sandalwood, patchouli and jasmine), and salt.

Before you begin the ritual itself, it's time to prepare the salt solution. Bring your chalice to the altar full of water. Stir in a tablespoon of salt, then hold your hands, palms down, above the water as you ritually chant the Salt and Water Protective Invocation:

SALT AND WATER PROTECTIVE INVOCATION

Salt in water, by casting thee
No spell nor unknown purpose be
Except in true accord with me.
And as my will, so mote it be!

As you chant, feel the power of your words flowing through your hands into the solution. Let's set the stage for all our ritual work by saying that a parrot wouldn't be good at it. It is the *feeling* that you generate that provides the impetus and power for creation of that which *You Will*. Without the *feeling* of power as you chant, your rituals will be dead and you can't expect good results. So practice until you can chant with power in your voice and feeling in your inner being—this is the secret of infinite personal power. When you feel that it is finished, you are ready to start the complete altar consecration ritual.

How to Consecrate Your Altar and Working Ritual Areas

The ritual begins with the sprinkling of the salt water you have just prepared. Dip your fingers into the solution and sprinkle it liberally, first around the corners of the room and then on and around your altar and meditation area. While you are sprinkling the solution, keep repeating the Salt and Water Protective Invocation, "Salt in water. . . ." When the room is well sprinkled put the chalice back on your altar, light your incense and put it in the incense burner. Now sit down at your altar and light the candles. Then hold your hands with the palms facing the candle flames in the classic benediction pose and chant the Fire Elemental Invocation:

FIRE ELEMENTAL INVOCATION

Creatures of fire, this charge I give,
No evil in my presence live,

No phantom, spook, nor spell may stay
   Around   us place, not night nor day.
Hear my will addressed to thee,
   And as my word, so mote it be.

When you feel the power of the Fire Elemental Invocation, you're ready to anoint your altar (and your own brow if you didn't do it in preparation for this ceremony) with exorcism oil. Put a little oil on the end of your finger and make a small cross of it on each of the four corners of your altar and in the center and chant the Air Elemental Invocation:

AIR ELEMENTAL INVOCATION

And now this oily essence fair
   Adds its great power to the air
Attracting spirits of the Light
   Protecting us both day and night.
This charge is true and proper, see.
   And as my will, so mote it be.

This brings us to the point of actual dedication, binding or consecration of your altar and its place. Again with arms raised and palms facing forward in the classic manner of benediction, feel the power flowing to purify and exorcise your place of meditation and ritual work as you chant the Altar Consecration Chant:

ALTAR CONSECRATION CHANT

Elementals, Spirits, Gods of old,
   This altar fresh we now behold.
You all agree it's bound to me
   In peace and true serenity.
I charge you to assist e'ermore,
   That Light and Love shall be our store.
This place IS perfect harmony.
   And as my will, so mote it be.

You are now ready for meditation or special occult and witchcraft work. But always remember, before leaving your altar *dismiss the elementals.* Speak your words firmly *aloud:* "All elemental spirits gathered here, I thank you for your help and participation. Now go in peace back to your native habitats and harm no one on your way. Thank you also to the wonderful spirit beings who have participated and who help me always."

Now one word before we turn to the art of meditation. A good Witch is certainly an eclectic—I'll remind you of this many times. We have given you a protective ritual and a consecration ritual, but you will find other uses for parts of these ceremonies. Put the various chants and uses of ritual together in many trial combinations to find the things that generate the most feeling and power for you. Finally you will evolve your own set of personal rituals based on your experience and demonstrated *results*. The challenge is to experiment and try—but also to carefully observe the effects in your daily existence. When you see all facets of your life suddenly improving, you are convinced for all time of the power of White Witchcraft.

How Unexpected Benefits Happened to S.F.

Much practical good can come from the altar consecration ritual by itself. Here is a report from S.F.: "I wondered if I should go ahead with my altar consecration ritual because there was a terrible pain in my left arm. But I decided to try. By the time I completed the ritual, the pain was gone and it has stayed away ever since. Perhaps even nicer, there is a new feeling of love in my house. My husband has become especially attentive and loving—he even remarked on how warm and loving he feels in the house now. You can be sure I will use the ritual at least monthly. I like the results."

THE ART OF MEDITATION AND HOW TO USE IT

Meditation is one of the most abused words in the language, but it is very important. Let's think of its useful power as a process of wooing or courting. At the point in your ritual work when you have invited the nature spirits and elementals to be present, there comes the task of building a true love affair. Think of the great advantage of carrying on a love affair with the potent forces of nature herself! What other people call "good luck," you will recognize as the simple response of the happy non-human, but never the less *real* spirit forces of nature.

The Power of Love in Effective Meditation

Thus the type of meditation we seek is the establishing of a love affair with life itself. As you sit peacefully at your altar, send love from your heart to life in all of its forms. Mentally feast on ideas of the beauty and richness of nature—let your thoughts explore the intricacies of love, cooperation, fertility, beauty, serenity, happiness, inner peace and good humor. Let the childlike feelings of wonder and awe build up within you as you contemplate the simplicity yet complexity of a force that can send a blade of grass through four inches of concrete to see the sun or generate 100 mile per hour winds in a hurricane. Contemplate the wonderous intelligence that built your fantastically efficient body one tiny cell at a time—and that keeps you in trim by replacing worn out cells to keep you strong and vital year after glorious year. *And love it!* Keep it up until the wonder, awe and love build up to a happy peak and you *feel a response!* You may literally feel yourself being petted, there may be balls of light seen dancing around you, or you may just feel a powerful peace. But court this feeling, *it is the power you will use for all your spells and accomplishments.*

How a Magic Touch Was Acquired with Meditation

Just touching this response from the elemental and nature spirits can start a chain of happy coincidences and "good luck"! After one real touch of the power, Louise B. reported to us, "That power is the most! I carry it with me everywhere. Hope it doesn't wear out. When I returned a juicer to a large department store, the usually disdainful clerks bustled around getting my refund fast. They patted my shoulders and pointed out a few more faults with the same. We have a new miracle switchboard in my office which does everything except get numbers. Can't move without stepping on a telephone company big shot or engineer. But I always get my numbers. I'm the envy of my colleagues. They want to know how I acquire my magic touch!"

Let your meditation periods add that "magic touch" to your life. Modify the consecration ritual to keep it short and comfortable, then spend ten minutes in meditation. Just one short week can bring the magic back into all your activities!

How to Keep Your Aura Clean and Bright to Enhance Your Effectiveness

Let's consider Louise's hope that "it doesn't wear out." Remember this is literally a love affair. If you give it the consideration and interest that keeps it alive, it need never wear out. But if you treat your lover shabbily, the lustre of the romance will surely fade. Now how shall we apply this to your love affair with life?

From the occult standpoint the answer must be to keep your aura clean and bright. The aura is the self luminous energy field that is the real you. Later in the book we'll discuss methods of seeing it, but here we're just concerned with keeping it clean enough to enhance your love affair with life so the power doesn't "wear out." This is done by basic positive thinking and harmlessness. When your mood is happy and light and you are guilt-free, your aura is bright and lovely. Anything that makes you feel good helps to brighten your aura, but feelings of unworthiness or guilt, disgust or bitterness work just like dumping soot on a white rug.

Strive for a new overall attitude of peaceful coexistence with all of creation and it will put fresh magnetism in your aura to attract happy magical experiences and repel the unhappy kind. It works for all who honestly try it! We have spend very few words on this most important subject. Let's close the section with the reminder that anytime you sense the magic going out of your life, that's the signal to turn back to the aura cleaning process. The first and third chapters of my book, *Helping Yourself with ESP* are full of powerful aura-cleaning techniques for you who feel the need of more background. The trick is to turn to the basics of positive thinking—and really *eliminate the negative!* Do whatever you feel necessary, but keep that aura clean and bright—then I can guarantee the success of your cermonial magic and spell casting.

How to Construct Your Own Spells and Incantations

Thoughout this book we will suggest spells and rituals that include chants (or incantations), herbs, oils, powders and all the lore of historical witchcraft. But the best results will come for you as you learn to inject your own personality into the work. Nobody else's "carned" ritual will work perfectly for you. What worked for Solomon, Crowley, Merlin or the Witch of Endor drew its effectiveness from the power of the individual's personality. To work for you, it may require adjustment to blend more intelligently with the miracle that is *you*. Particularly in the work of incantations, the words must have rich meaning to *you* or they will not generate the power necessary to successful ritual work.

So let's talk about constructing or revising your own chants and spells. My dictionary defines spell as a *set of words believed to have magical power.* Indeed in this work you must believe that your words will reach and influence the forces you seek to manipulate. You can't try this "tongue in cheek" and expect results, yet balance reminds us that the heavy approach may bring results beyond what we'd like to experience. As always, effectiveness is somewhere in between—it's the *light touch* that feels the right amount of power to use that always wins.

Principal Gods of the Ancients Used as Sources of Energy

Since witchcraft antedates Christianity, its appeals were directed to the ancient gods now called "pagan." Whether or not you believe in the actual existence of such gods, you know that millions of people have prayed to them over the centuries and thus build up a vast store of really powerful energy. To use this energy is quite as scientific and practical as the drilling of wells to tap nature's stored up energy that we call oil.

There is a striking similarity between the functions of the gods of the various ancient peoples. The individual Germanic, Roman, Greek, Egyptian and Babylonian gods controlled their special facets of human life, and their *thoughtforms* are ready to work with *you* today. Table 2-1, titled Principal Gods of the Ancients, lists the special areas of interest of the important ancient deities. In planning a spell or incantation, the order of approach is to invoke the deity or a group of deities concerned with the area of your desire, then work in an appeal to the nature spirits and/or elementals in the same basic energy category, and close with the request or command to fulfill your desire.

In general the gentle touch that woos rather than tries to push the elementals around produces the happiest set of results in the long run. Try the light touch first and increase the power as you find it necessary to succeed. On the following page are a few sample chants that have been used effectively for centuries in combination with the oils and herbs as discussed in our next chapter. Begin to get the *feel* of spell casting as you study these and prepare to make them your own.

Table 2-1: Principal Gods of the Ancients

	Germanic	Roman	Greek	Egyptian	Babylonian
Supreme God	Woden; Frigg	Jupiter; Juno	Zeus; Hera	Ra	Marduk
Creator				Ptah	Anu
Sky	Frigg	Jupiter	Uranua; Zeus	Nut	Anu; Anshar
Sun		Apollo	Helios	Ra	Shamash
Moon		Diana	Artemis	Thoth	Sin
Earth	Sif	Tellus	Gaea	Geb	Enlil
Air					Enlil
Fire	Hoenir	Vulcan	Hephaestus		Girru
Sea	Niord	Neptune	Poseidon		
Water and Rain	Thor	Jupiter	Zeus	Tefnut	Ea
Light	Balder	Apollo	Apollo		
Thunder	Thor	Jupiter	Zeus		Adad
Wind			Aeolus	Amen	Marduk
Storm		Jupiter	Zeus		Adad
Dawn		Aurora	Eos		
Mother Goddess	Nerthus	Venus	Aphrodite	Isis	Ishtar
Fertility	Frey	Bona Dea	Rhea	Osiris	
Harvests	Balder	Saturn	Cronos		
Vegetation	Balder	Ceres	Adonis	Osiris	Tammuz
Death	Hel	Pluto	Hades	Osiris	Nergal
Music and Poetry	Bragi		Apollo	Thoth	
Wisdom and Learning	Nimir	Minerva	Athena	Thoth	Nebo
War	Tiu	Mars; Bellona	Ares; Athena		
Love	Freya	Cupid	Eros		
Messenger	Hermod	Mercury	Hermes		
Healing	Eira	Apollo	Apollo		Gula
Hunting	Uller	Diana	Artemis		
Wine		Liber	Dionysus		
Divine Smith and Artificer	Mimir	Vulcan	Hephaestus		

SAMPLE CHANTS FOR SPECIFIC PURPOSES

Chant to Attract a Lover

> Venus, Cupid, Eros, Friends,
>> Your help will serve my rightful ends.
> My loving trust appeals to thee,
>> Please send my true love straight to me.

Chant to Enhance an Existing Love Affair

> Aphrodite, Venus, Ishtar, Isis,
>> Keep our love and bring no crisis.

Chant for Business Improvement

> Nature spirits of the air,
>> Bring us business and to spare.
> We serve them well as you do see,
>> So this request is right for thee.

Chant for Good Luck

> Oh wondrous spirits of Pan and Puck,
>> I turn to you for much good luck.
> This herb maintains our contact pure
>> And brings good luck that's swift and sure.

It will be best to wait until you finish the next chapter before using these or the chants that you will begin to construct for yourself. When used with the right feeling and oneness with nature, they will indeed produce miracles for you and your loved ones.

CHAPTER POINTS TO REMEMBER

1) Practice the protection ritual and make it feel good before entering into any other ritual work or ceremonial magic.

2) Next use the altar consecration ritual not just as a ceremony but as your beginning of establishing a love affair with life.

3) The love affair meditation practiced regularly will add a touch of magic to your whole life and start you on your personal path of success.

4) Harmlessness and positive thinking are the soap and water used to keep your aura clean and bright. This is the way to bring success to all your ritual work and keep your magic love affair with life fresh and alive.

5) Study the idea and feeling of the sample incantations with the purpose of constructing special purpose chants and spells of your own.

6) Whether or not you believe in the actual existence of the ancient gods, the power of centuries of accumulated prayer energy and expectation of results is available to your properly constructed spell just as oil is to the scientific drilling operation.

7) Study the use of herbs and oils (Chapter 3) before you use the sample chants given here.

Chapter Three

How to Enhance Your Spells with Herbs, Oils, Candles and Incense

*T*he evolving or developing Witch quickly learns that there is a good deal more to the world than meets the untrained eye. There is a great complexity of elementary and spirit beings that indeed do enter into the activites of men in many subtle but highly effective ways. To know these beings, even in part, is to stand on the threshold of limitless personal power.

HOW TO UNDERSTAND THE KINGDOM
OF ELEMENTARY SPIRITS AND THEIR POWERS

The ancient concepts of the four elements, *Earth, Water, Fire* and *Air* has a living reality in Witchcraft because it gives us the key to unlock a fantastic power. Don't confuse this with the scientific elements of chemistry. The elements of Witchcraft are living personalities which have dominion over their material counter-parts. To distinguish the living spirit personalities from the matter which they control, the term *elemental* or *elemental spirit* is applied. The elementals will cooperate with you in magnificently practical ways when you approach them properly. In the history of Witchcraft you will find two different methods of approach, *command* and *friendship.* I will stick to the friendship method in this book because the downfall of too many has resulted from the revolution that is a natural result of excessive command. Friendship with the elemental spirits is completely safe and generally more effective in gaining your favors and "good fortune." Since we want the elementals to be our friends, we will need to know more about them.

The Earth Elementals are known as *Gnomes* or *Trolls,* and their leader's name is *Gob*. These happy spirits are entrusted with the treasures of the earth such as jewels, gold, silver and platinum. They are attracted by perfumed salts and powders in combination with happy incantations. In Chapter 7 we will have much more to say about the financially rewarding methods of wooing them.

The Water Elementals are called *Nymphs* or *Undines,* and their leader's name is *Neckna.* They are the essence of plant life and their enthusiastic help will raise prize-winning roses or double the output of a cornfield. You will find them intimately associated with healing rituals for plants, animals and humans. Naturally they are attracted by water solutions and herb washes. The water elementals also cooperate with the earth elements to bring prosperity to the well disciplined Witch. We will encounter them often as our work unfolds.

The Air Elementals are called *Sylphs* or *Zephyrs.* They are the spreaders of knowledge and fresh ideas because they travel far and wide, and they will bring you a friendly breeze whenever you politely ask them to. Their leader's name is *Paralda.* They are attracted by incense, perfume oils, colognes, and well-constructed incantations. The muse of the poet, writer or artist is directly connected to the air elementals, and this source of inspiration and information is limitless.

The Fire Elementals are called *Salamanders.* They are the least interested in humans of all the elementals, but their firey nature can be most helpful in clearing away obstacles of a psychological or psychic nature. Their leader's name is *Djin.* They are attracted by the fire of candles, charcoal, and incense. Well-rhymed incantations may induce them to burn away your psychic troubles without touching a hair of your head.

This gives us the information for a table that will be useful for ready reference in your regular work with the elemental spirits. You will find it engraved in your mind soon enough, but for the present let's recap it:

THE ELEMENTAL SPIRITS

Element	*Name of Spirits*	*Leader*	*Attracted by*	*Rulers of*
Earth	Gnomes or Trolls	Gob	Salts and powders	Riches and treasure
Water	Nymphs or Undines	Neckna	Washes and solutions	Plants and healing

Element	Name of Spirits	Leader	Attracted by	Rulers of
Air	Sylphs or Zephyrs	Paralda	Oils and incense	Knowledge and inspiration
Fire	Salamanders	Djin	Fire and incense	Freedom and change

As you develop your natural instinct about which element or group of elements to bring to bear on any particular problem, you will find some tendency in your personality to favor one approach over the other. This generally ties in to your own astrological sun sign, for instance: The fire signs, Aries, Leo and Sagittarius are full of fire, drive and expansiveness; the air signs, Gemini, Libra and Aquarius are versatile and hard to corner like air itself and tend to shift direction like the wind; the water signs are sensitive but persistent and flow on to their goals over, under and around the obstacles; the earth signs, Taurus, Virgo and Capricorn are the steady but somewhat stubborn people who are quite earthy but also down to earth in their doings. We'll go into rituals for invocation of and gaining cooperation from the elementals in our next chapter.

Meanwhile, let's begin to approach the use of herbs, oils, powders, candles and incense as strong attractors of the elemental and nature spirit powers of our great unseen world. We'll begin with the herbs. They are often used in combination, and you will develop the feel of this part of the work as you experiment, but let's start with a general list of herbs and their traditional uses:

BASIC HERBS ASSOCIATED WITH

Health	Love	Prosperity	Protection
Vervain	Basil leaves	Cinnamon	Vetivert powder
Thyme	Cubeb berries	Yellow Dock	Boldo leaves
Sassafras	Orris root	Squill root	Mandrake root
Peppermint	Spikeweed	John the Conqueror	Garlic
Horehound	Vanillin	Silver Weed	Snakehead
Hops	Vervain	Jezebel root	Gilead buds
Eucalyptus	Violet powder	Prince's Pine	Stone root
Feverfew	Laurel	Red Clover	Basil
Asafaetida	Myrtle	Buckeye	Bay leaves
Catnip	Absinthe	Iris Moss	Asafaetida

HOW TO USE THE HERBS—
INFUSIONS, DECOCTIONS, SEASONING, WASHES, INCENSES

Our students have a common reaction at this point: "So here's a nice list of herbs, but what do I do with them?" We will go into detail on the subjects of health, love, money and protection in individual chapters. So let's answer the question in general terms here. This is a "get familar with them" discussion. How would you expect to use an herb? Herb tea immediately comes to mind as a starting point.

Infusion is the Witchcraft term for an herb tea designed for a special purpose. Teas are made in the normal manner by pouring boiling water over the leaves or flowers, about 1/2 ounce of the herb mixture to a cup of water. Let it steep for about five minutes while using the proper incantation over it, then strain, sweeten with honey if you like and serve it to yourself, your lover, etc. Herbs like sassafras, sarsaprilla and peppermint make quite palatable teas, but many other herbs do too. You will learn to ask an herb if it will work in your planned infusion, etc. and get a useful answer. But that comes later.

Decoction is the Witchcraft term for a tea like substance made by boiling the hard parts, such as the stems, roots and bark of your herbs, Some of these can be used as a tea, but most are used for a wash or to soak a cloth or piece of towel to apply to the skin or perhaps leave under your front porch.

Wash is the Witchcraft term for an herb and water mixture used to wash down or sprinkle a floor, mailbox, etc. as part of your spell casting. A decoction can also be used as a wash. You will find many spells that use an herb soaked in water and chanted over for three, seven or nine days before being used as a wash. Care is necessary in planning your own wash mixtures to avoid a mouldy, mildewy mess. But again you will learn to talk to the herbs and get sound advice on how to use them.

Incenses are another big stock in trade of Witchcraft, and the herbs enter into most of the formulations. We will give several recipes for making your own incenses as we go deeper into the work.

Seasoning is also a wonderful tool of Witchcraft. And many of the favorite seasonings of good cooks also have occult uses. For instance basil used in a salad or cooked into a tasty dish and shared with a member of the opposite sex proves a strong stimulant to lasting love. But any one of these alone is relatively weak. It is as we put them together in combination with incantation and invocation of the proper elemental and nature spirit help that we build the working power.

This has been a purely introductory section, but necessary. We will build specific spells, and develop techniques for designing your own spells, out of the lore that we are slowly unfolding. And very shortly we'll get to the meat of the "how to."

How L.W. Exorcized Evil Influences from Business

L.W. owns a restaurant in North Carolina. Her business suddenly dropped off quite badly and there were several symptoms of black magic or negative occult practices being used against her. We sent her an herb mixture and the ritual you will learn in Chapter 9. Here is her report of results: "The last time I heard from you was when I received the #1 herbs and the ritual for exorcising evil entities. I feel sure you know what the prescription was used for, since you picked it for me. The situation was instantly healed, and business is now better than ever before."

How Herb Techniques Helped Tina A. Get Married

Tina A. had been going with John for 18 months. She was thinking marriage, and had been for way over a year, but John never quite seemed to get around to popping the magic question. Then as she reported: "Nothing logical I had tried seemed to do any good, so I invited John to dinner. Naturally I was wearing my finest love oil perfume, but I think it was the herb cooking that turned the trick. The salad was full of basil and I used oregano, basil and bay laurel in a dish I called 'Tina Stew.' After dinner, John smiled at me and said, 'I get the feeling that it's time to get married and settle down with you. How about it?' I don't have to tell you my answer! We are very happy."

How to Make and Use the Witch Oils

The basic essential oils are readily available at your local occult, curiosity, or antique shop—there are many of these all over the country. Should you experience difficulty in obtaining any of the items mentioned in this book, write to me care of E.S.P. Laboratory, 7559 Santa Monica Blvd., Los Angeles, Calif. 90046, and I'll be happy to suggest one or more suppliers. Let's begin by suggesting the perfume oils traditionally used for attracting:

Love	Prosperity	Protection	Friendly Nature Spirits	Health
Jasmine	Frankessence	Sandalwood	Lime	Rose
Rose	Myrrh	Patchouli	Carnation	Carnation
Lavendar	Musk	Citron	Gardenia	Citron
Frankessence	Rose	Jasmine	Wintergreen	Gardenia

It's normal to use the essential oils in combination with each other and with herbal oils that you have made yourself. To make your own herbal oils, start with a good vegetable oil base (a safflower or corn oil as used for salads will do). Ritually crush the herbs in your mortar and pestle and stir them into your oil base. Store the mixture is a previously exorcised dark place. Traditionally, you would chant over your mixture each evening for nine days. Then you bring it out, and chant over it again as you strain it. You can get a tremendous amount of power into an herbal oil with the proper feeling and power in your chanting. Then with the right ritual—look out world! You will find many herb oil recipes in the chapters that follow.

A Favorable Business Experience with Using Witch Oil

Even by themselves, the oils do a good job of getting things off of a dead spot. Let's look at a report from Corrine F.: "That prosperity oil works wonders! The first day I wore it to work at the TV store I sold two color TV sets in one hour! If it keeps up like this—my money worries are over"! And she has reported regular financial improvement many times since.

How to Make the Witch's Powders

The witch's powders are assoicated with attracting the earthy nature spirits and elementals for their tangible help. Ritual combining of the ingredients in your mortar and pestle with feeling in your chant can build great power and attract the aid of these helpful beings. Here are sample recipes for a couple of the most often used witch powders:

Money Drawing Powder	Love Drawing Powder
1 oz. Sandalwood Powder	1 oz. Sandalwood Powder
1/2 dram Frankessence oil	1/4 tsp. Cinnamon
1/4 dram Patchouli oil	1 tsp. Sweet Basil
1/4 dram Myhrr oil	1 tsp. Myrtle
1/4 tsp. Cinnamon	1/2 dram Frankessence oil
1 tsp. Yellow Dock	3/8 drams Jasmine oil
4 oz. Talc	1/8 dram Patchouli oil
	4 oz. Talc

Combine your ingredients while using the proper chant (see Chapter 6 and 7). The trick to making your powders is to combine all the liquid and solid ingredients except the talc and get them well mixed. The sandalwood and herbs will absorb the oils and afterwards carry their fragrance into the talc mixture. But because it will not absorb any of your liquid, be sure to add the talc last. You will find many good uses for your powders in sachets or sprinkled in the right places to attract your good fortune.

How M.S. Used a Money-Drawing Powder

M.S. runs a mail order business as her sole source of livelihood. She tested the money—drawing powder formula given here along with the chant that we will present in Chapter 7. Here is her report: "I tried making the money drawing power and using it with the ritual chant over my mailbox somewhat skeptically. Immediately my business picked up by more than 25 percent and seemed to stay there for several weeks. Then I decided this must be just a coincidence and discountinued using the powder and ritual. Immediately my business dropped back to a bit less than it had been before the experiment, and it stayed there for two weeks. When I went back to the ritual, business picked right up again. I'll never stop using it now!"

How to Make Incenses

There are many good incenses on the market, but the expert in any work wants the knowledge and ability to do it for himself (or herself), just as is true with making the powders, oils, etc. Depending on the degree of importance you attach to the ritual of preparation, you may powder your own herbs or buy them in the ready to use state. In the recipes that follow, we assume that your herbs are already powdered. Here are sample incense formulations for reasonably small quantities of incense to:

Attract Perfect Mate	Attract Psychic Phenomena
1/2 oz. Sweet Bugle	1/4 oz. Bayberry
1/2 oz. Cinnamon	1/2 oz. Sandalwood Powder
1 oz. Sandalwood powder	1/4 oz. Anise seed
1/4 oz. Anise seed	1/8 tsp. Saltpeter
1/8 tsp. Saltpeter	1/2 oz. Patchouli oil
1/4 oz. Frankessence	1 oz. Myhrr
7 oz. Powdered Charcoal	7 oz. Powdered Charcoal
6 oz. Tincture of Benzoin	6 oz. Tincture of Benzoin

Now that we have given you an arsenal of physical tools, the next step is to learn to combine them under the direction of your constructive will and the inspiration of your creative imagination to get what you want. Indeed your wildest dream can be brought to reality when you become expert in operating the techniques in the following chapters. Recipes for tested prosperity and love incenses will be given to you in the appropriate chapters.

Reports on Usage of Love Incense

I'd like to share this comment from L.B. about our research in incense: "I gave my cleaning lady a sample of the Love Attracting Incense. She burned some in the presence of her very old stud cat. She told me that she was amazed at the effect it had on him, and she hopes it will do as well with her husband." A later happy report says it did!

Here is another report from our field research in the incenses: "The Prosperity/Love incense smells nice. Since I have been burning it around the house our family has seemed more in a loving mood. There seems to be more harmony and lately we have had more friends drop in on us. I've burned it in my bedroom and my money supply has increased in a comfortable way."—J.S., Canada.

CHAPTER POINTS TO REMEMBER

1) Tremendous help is available to all who understand the kingdom of elemental spirits and learn to work with them.

2) Develop the natural instinct that tells you which elemental to evoke for the specific purpose you seek to achieve.

3) Herbal lore is a major asset of Witchcraft. Study the table of basic herbs and get the feel of using herbs.

4) Both perfume and herbal oils have great value in your coming work, and besides they smell good. Get used to using the oils and odors to enhance your Witchcraft.

5) Similarly, the powders and incenses are wonderful tools to attract the elementals and bring much good to you.

6) When you learn to put all your tools together you will discover that you have the power to bring your fondest dreams into living reality.

Chapter Four

How to Gain the Cooperation of "Familiar Spirits" and the "Little People"

*E*ssential to your progress in becoming an effective Witch is a knowledge of the reality of non-physical entities. There are two broad classes of entity (or spirit being) life both of which are important to the success of your work. We will call the entities that you build or create yourself, *thoughtforms*. The other type of entity already has a life of its own—these are the elementals, nature spirits, and the spirit beings who have lived a normal life in a physical human body but now are called *dead*. The most significant difference between the two types of beings is simply that you *build thoughtforms*, but you must attract or court the spirit beings. Since the occult purpose of much ritual work is to build a *thoughtform* that performs a specific task for you, we will begin this chapter with the study of *thoughtforms*.

THOUGHTFORMS—WHAT THEY ARE AND HOW TO BUILD THEM

In our Basic Protection Ritual work, we spoke of building a living entity whose sole reason for existence is to protect you. At the time you may have dismissed the statement as a bit of over-exuberance on my part, but you will find that it is *literally* true. The real power of your ritual work will come as you learn to build a fully living entity by moulding the energy generated by your creative imagination with your constructive will. The basic tecnhique for building a living entity that becomes your *thoughtform* servant requires practice, but the effort will prove well worth it to you. The traditional method involves the energy of your hands, your heart and your mind.

Hold your hands a comfortable distance in front of you with the palms facing each other. Let your fingers curl in a relaxed manner and bring your hands together until your finger tips are about two inches apart. Now *will* the vital energy to flow between your hands and *feel* an energy field build up between them. (Even a slight sensation of heat or tingling indicates that the energy is flowing in response to your direction.) As the energy builds in power, begin to program it by projecting your clearly formed thought into it from your mind while you add love energy from your heart. Picture your thought (the realization of your desire) clearly in the energy field between your hands, thus it is easy to love. Continue to program and love the energy field until you feel it take on a life of its own. Then you can release it in love to gather the physical matter it needs to manifest.

How F.S. Found an Apartment She Wanted

F.S. found a wonderful new job, but it was way on the "other side of town." Because of the pressure of family obligations, she felt there was no time to look for a new apartment. So that night she built a *thoughtform* and visualized the apartment she wanted, complete with large rooms and plenty of light and air. When she got off work on the new job the next afternoon, there was an urge to drive around for a moment in the new neighborhood. Sure enough, there was a for rent sign in front of a two-story duplex. When she went inside, she saw the rooms exactly as she had visualized the night before—it was complete even to the swimming pool in the back and plenty of privacy, and at *a price she could afford.* The *thoughtform* had led her unerringly to exactly the place she wanted. It works wonders for all who use it, but guidance is only one tiny application. As the book unfolds, you will find many wonderful uses for *your thoughtforms.* Here is another very useful *thoughtform* application:

A Watcher Thoughtform—and How to Build it

A *watcher thoughtform* is much more than a concept. It is a living entity, built out of your own *thoughtform* substance with an independent existence all its own as an auxiliary set of eyes and ears for you. The unusual nature of the six-foot experimental pyramid in our E.S.P. Laboratory Lobby entered into an experience of "proof" to a man stationed on a ship in the North Atlantic. He sent his watcher to have a look at our Lab in Los Angeles and wrote us this report: "My watcher made a trip to your Lab and gave me some interesting observations. The highlight of its comment was, 'this big white pyramid shaped thing down there had the strangest energy currents in it, the weird thing almost sucked me into it' "!

There are practical uses of all sorts to a watcher. For instance, they are wonderful at helping you with difficult shopping. Marla O. wanted a crystal ball as much for a conversation piece as for psychic work, but she was short of time for such frivolous shopping. So she gave her watcher the task of locating her crystal ball, specifying size and acceptable price. On her next day off, she was running the usual errands when she found herself walking into a small shop that was strange to her. There in a box marked "Sale—all items in this box $6.00," she saw a lovely four-inch crystal ball. It was a close-out sale of an item that normally sells in the $40 price range. Marla almost considers that crystal ball a gift from her watcher. You can be sure it received an extra feeding of thanks and love that evening.

But the easiest way to understand the value of a watcher is to build one for yourself. My watcher is about the size of a volleyball. It's soft and fuzzy and almost all eyes and ears. That is so it can be most efficient in gathering information as I may need it. The technique for building your watcher is part of the standard *thoughtform* building work we will use in much of the ritual work throughout this book. So let's study the process in detail. The ritual begins by setting your protection, for instance with the basic protection ritual. Be sure that you are relaxed and serene and your attitude is positive and light—you wouldn't want to create a monster. If you are agitated when you build it, your watcher will seek out only agitation and confusion to bring back to you.

The *thoughtform* is built by holding your hands out in front of you about six inches apart with the palms facing each other as if you were holding a volleyball. *Will* the psychic energy to flow between your hands and build a living entity while you send love from your heart and power from your eyes to the area between your hands. As you feel the energy begin to flow, form your watcher with the watcher building chant:

WATCHER BUILDING CHANT

Thought of purity and light,
   Fresh life I bring to you tonight.
Ears to hear and eyes to see,
   My faithful watcher you will be,
Watching for me far and near,
   What I should know, that you will hear.
Gather all effectively,
   And bring it quickly back to me.
Execute this faithfully,
   And as my word, so mote it be!

As to the number of times to repeat the chant, how long does it take you to "see" it take shape and form? The touch will be subtle of course, but you should be able to reach out and *feel* the *reality* of your new friend living as a *thoughtform*. The standard number of times to chant for this purpose is nine, but you may enjoy feeding your *thoughtform* watcher with the energy many more times. As long as the chant is powerful and alive, and you feel energy flowing into your new being, it's fine to work on it. Also, one day may not see the full strength given to your new thought being, so repeating the ritual for three, seven or nine consecutive nights is good. The reality must be so well built that you can call your watcher friend to you and touch it, knowing exactly where it is and feeling its enjoyment of the attention. I like to whistle to mine and have it perch on my right shoulder where I pet it and it whispers information into my right ear at the same time. You should regularly call your watcher to you to give it instructions— tell it what types of ideas and information you need, and regularly praise if for its good work.

The need for secrecy is obvious in your watcher work, particularly as you get attached to the powerful thing. The average person will think you're crazy or just putting them on, while others may react with fear and resentment. So keep it to yourself, but a watcher is a useful household tool—soon you will wonder how you ever got along without it.

How to Maintain Contact and Control over Your Watcher

Regular communication with your watcher is the only way to get the benefit of this *thoughtform* building effort. As we progress, you will learn to build other *thoughtforms* for many different purposes, so the monitoring work we learn here will be useful to much of our future Witchcraft. You can tell what kind of a day you're apt to have by holding a regular morning conference with your watcher. At least once a day you should call it in for a friendly meeting—the more you think of your *thoughtforms* as useful entities (or people) the more good you will derive from them. If you feel short of time, you can use a very short version of the basic protection ritual to be comforatble. Then use this simple chant to summon your friend:

WATCHER CONFERENCE CHANT

Watcher, watcher, come to me
    And tell me of the things you see.
What's in store for this fine day
    Bring true guidance right away.
All you know, now tell to me,
    And as my will, so mote it be!

Then *feel* your friendly *thoughtform* hop on your shoulder, and listen as it whispers words of wisdom in your ear. To some there will be an actual voice, but most of us get our report as an intuitive feeling or flow of thoughts. If you become uncomfortable at what you feel or hear, don't leave your altar until you have gone through a cleansing ritual (our Altar Consecration Ritual will do for now) to get the negativity safely washed out of your aura.

How an Accident Was Avoided with Thoughtforms

An example of help from a watcher was reported by D.H. She told us: "At my morning ritual my watcher warned me of danger in traffic. So I went through the aura cleansing and protection ritual with great care. Later in the day I was driving a friend's Cadillac and a car came skidding across the road right at me. But it missed the Cadillac and hit somebody else. I gave my Watcher a couple of extra words of thanks when I got home. That protective *thoughtform* is priceless"!

How to Contact the "Little People"

The folklore of the world is full of "Little people"—Fairies, Leprechauns, Gremlins, Gnomes, Trolls, Nymphs, Sylphs, Genies,

Elves and the friendly Gronkydoddles we meet at E.S.P. Laboratory cavort in legend and indeed in real life. Let's use the broad term *Nature Spirit* to include all the elemental spirits and "little people." There is a great deal of solid help waiting for those who approach the nature spirits with the right attitude. After using the ritual we are about to present, C.N. happily reported: "I have had many beautiful experiences, but this was my first materialization! I was dressing hurriedly yesterday morning and finding a button missing decided to use a pin and hide it under a scarf. This morning I prepared to *steal* a button from a less conspicuous place. I was deliberating when suddenly from a space in front of me (about 1 1/2 feet away) something bounced into my lap. It was a (or the) button I needed. Needless to say I was startled, then amazed, but I remembered to thank the nature spirits for their help."

How a Job Was Found

O.J. had experienced great difficulty in finding the right job. After making friends with the nature spirits he reported this result: "Have had wonderful luck from the first time I used the ritual. I have had responses of more than enough to the jobs I previously applied for and then thought I was the forgotten man, only to have now the mail reply or inquiry as to my availability arrive when I would least expect it. The instances and/or incidents on the plus or positive side are too many not to give credit where it is due. I *believe* in the Power of *Thoughtforms* is about the only thing I can say, and nothing now can make me disbelieve."

How to Have Good Luck with Ritual

How shall we get you on the path to the "good luck" that the nature spirits can easily bring you? The starting point is the love affair with life that we began in our first chapter. Now we will extend the love affair to include the nature spirits. You'll find this by far the best approach—some people order the little people around with great assumed authority, but they react by carefully taking you literally and doing exactly what you told them to do, not what you want them to! Those of your who are experienced in computer programming will understand the dangers here. So unless your logic is always completely flawless in every detail, there's only one way to go, and this is a nature spirit courting ritual.

Before you begin the ritual, set your attitude as one of good-natured friendship toward the little people. Begin by setting your protection with the basic protection ritual or your own embellished version. Light your candles and use the Attract Psychic Phenomena incense as we described in Chapter 3. Then anoint your brow and the back of your neck with one of the nature spirit attracting oils (your choice of lime, carnation, gardenia or wintergreen), and use the Nature Spirit Invocation:

NATURE SPIRIT INVOCATION

Little people everywhere,
  Your fun and love I seek to share.
Gronkydoddles hear my call,
  Leprechauns come one and all.

Leader, Gob, of Gnome and Troll,
  Come and share your humor droll.
Neckna and your Undines, bold,
  Play with me your games of old.

Paralda, Zephryrs of the air,
  Caress me while my skin is bare.
Salamanders led by Djin,
  The candle flames you may play in.

Nature spirits of all sort
  In friendship let us now cavort.
A child of love for you I'll be,
  My mood is light as you can see.

And always as you sing and play,
  I feel my problems fade away.
Your laughter, love and fun come through
  And help me feel alive like you.

Use the chant several times, then relax and be alert to the happy response. You may feel something playing with your hair or touching parts of your body, there may be myriad of tiny dancing lights or rushes of wind all around you, objects on your altar may be wiggled or even levitated and moved around, you may hear voices or see pictures inside your head, or there may just be a good feeling about you. Don't be disappointed if there is not a bunch of wild phenomena, just enjoy whatever comes and be thankful for it. I often repeat the chant as much as eight or nine times, with long pauses between—you hate to stop when you're having a good time. Then when you are ready, close the ritual as we discussed in Chapter 2, taking special care to thank the elementals for their presence and *dismiss* them. After a few good sessions, you can be assured that good luck will follow you everywhere as part of your new friendship with the nature spirits.

How to Make Contact with Your Familiar Spirit

The useful idea of a Familiar Spirit relates to the class of entity that is already in existence and can be contacted for guidance and tangible help. Yes, we came to these bodies on the planet earth to build our own *thoughtform* servants and generally learn to stand on our own two feet. But it's a great comfort to be in contact with a spirit entity who has greater wisdom and perspective than you. At least such a being should be an excellent sounding board to try out your solutions to problems *before* you actually implement them. And so we find ourselves squarely up against the question, "How do I contact my familiar spirit (or spirit teacher)"?

I'd like to stress the importance of your own psychological condition at the time of your seeking. Too many people rush to their altars with minds full of garbage and complain that they are ignored and forsaken by all types of spirit-being help. Thus exorcism in its meaning of consecration is an important beginning. In the great occult tradition it is said that before the seeker can speak in the presence of the masters, the tongue must lose its power to wound—so if you want the joy of Witchcraft conversation, take heed. The lifting of your mental attitude and the general psychic atmosphere around you is the certain method of reaching the help we naturally seek.

We will shortly give you a ritual for contacting your Familiar Spirit, but first let's talk about motivation. Your seeking, particularly for the first few contacts, must be for rapport and companionship—this is not the time to ask your spirit friends to go into the kitchen and wash your dirty dishes! When you really need help, your spirit people *know* it, and gladly pitch in to clear away obstacles or bring the new job, lover, or opportunity that makes life good again. Let it work naturally as you build you new relationship.

In contacting the Familiar Spirit, we can expect great cooperation—you don't have to build up a *thoughtform*, the entity is real and normally eager for closer contact with you. A good system for making contact with your Spirit Teacher begins with the Altar Consecration Ritual that we used in Chapter 2. The actual consecration of the altar is optional, but after the invocation of the elementals and lighting of candles and incense, use the following "Call to Your Spirit Teacher":

CALL TO YOUR SPIRIT TEACHER

Oh, Teacher mine, I call to thee.
 I seek your guidance earnestly.
In silence now, I sit and listen
 For your Light and Love to glisten
All around me everywhere.
 I thank you for the good we share.

Chant it three times, then do what you said: *Sit and listen.* And it's a good idea to look, too, you may see the aura of your Familiar Spirit. Give it a good chance. If you are not up-tight, but are paying attention to the very subtle things, you will surely notice that there is a presence. And that's a big step because you can immediately say, "Welcome"! Greet the presence as a good friend and feel the heart to heart contact.

CONTACTING THE RIGHT SPIRIT TEACHER

Here the normal student asks: "How do you know you have contacted the right teacher"?

My answer would be, how do you know you have met a good teacher in a normal human body? Isn't it by the way they act and the ideas they impart to you? Another good consideration is your psychic and psychological condition when you tried for the first contact. The more completely spiritual you felt, the better the chance of contacting the real thing, not some joker imposter. Next comes the *feeling* of the presence—how does it make you feel? Oh yes, the first time or two, the hair may stand up on the back of your neck with fright, but we get past that stage very quickly, then how does the presence make you feel? If you are uplifted and inspired, that's a good recommendation. But if you come away with the urge to go shoot grandma or something, then break off that contact and try for another when you are more relaxed and peaceful.

The contact with your Spirit Teacher is another good time to extend the love affair with life concept to include this very helpful being. Reach out to share the Light and build a fresh rapport with the great realm of spirit beings. The benefits are as tangible as you expect them to be.

How G.H. Was Warned About a Suitor

G.H. was considering marriage for the third time, but was doubtful about the man who had proposed to her. She used the ritual to contact her spirit teacher and asked for guidance. Apparently nothing happened, so she went on to bed. The next day she bumped into her suitor in the street and had the feeling that he was a perfect stranger. Immediately the previous night's ritual work flashed into her mind and she knew she had received her answer. She broke off that relationship and soon met a man who was obviously much better suited to her. At last report they are very happily married.

Guidance, the doorway to a wonderful new job, spiritual unfoldment, and finding of the perfect mate or the answer to your most perplexing problem is as close as *your* altar and that happy contact with your Familiar Spirit. Use it and live life more fully than you have dared to dream possible!

CHAPTER POINTS TO REMEMBER

1) There are two types of spirit entity—*thoughtforms* that you build yourself, and spirits that you must attract. Practice the *thoughtform* building technique to gain a working proficiency.

2) You can build a *thoughtform* to act as your "watcher." It becomes a living entity whose sole purpose is to be your extra set of eyes and ears.

3) Use the ritual to build your watcher and stay in contact with it always—the ritual is easy and the benefits are great.

4) The little people or Nature Spirits are a source of boundless good luck. Use the ritual to establish a love affair with the Nature

Spirits and enjoy listening to your friends complain that you lead some sort of a charmed life.

5) The Familiar Spirit ritual will put you in contact with your own Spirit Teacher. This is a source of guidance and tangible help beyond the imagination of the average human being. The first contacts will prove the reality and value of this contact to you.

Chapter Five ⌐━━━▸

How to See Into the Future
with White Witchcraft

*W*hat does tomorrow hold for you? And the day after, the month after or the year after? Knowledge of the future, like the Holy Grail, has been a dream of mankind since the dawn of history. But while most people daydreamed about it, others applied their wit and intelligence to doing something about it—and many of these doers were Witches!

SEEING INTO THE FUTURE IS A NORMAL WITCH POWER

The pious among us will tell you that the use of future seeing ability for personal gain will cause your powers to diminish. But common sense will tell you that the statement is an exact equivalent of something like: "Using electricty to run a motor that performs work for you instead of powering your light bulbs will destroy your electrical circuits."—It's utter nonsense! Indeed we can safely say that one way to tell a true witch from the self-styled phony variety is by the degree of affluence. The true witch quietly and naturally lives the abundant life while the phony makes a lot of noise about it and lives close to poverty.

The term *divination* is used to describe seeing into the future, and its roots tell use clearly how it is done. Divination means *divine revelation,* and tradition is full of it. Great names of Greek philosophy such as Plato and Socrates spoke of prophecy as the "noblest of the arts." The Greek Oracle of Delphi is perhaps best known, but the Egyptians, Chaldeans, Babylonians, Chinese and virtually all ancient people and nations were guided by prophecy to richer, fuller lives. The universal powers tapped for prophecy have not diminished—they are available to help *you* now!

How a Couple Avoided Financial Loss

During the 1969/70 period of very tight money and slow real estate sales, Agnes and Charles R. decided to move to Phoenix to seek better economic opportunity than in the slumping Los Angeles area. Their house had been listed for sale for three months with hardly a nibble, when in mid-Feburary, Agnes got the urge to move anyway. She said, "Let's go on and not be locked in this area just because of an old house." So they sought some prophetic help as part of the decision-making process. The I Ching divination gave them the hexagram reading "Keeping Still," but Agnes wasn't convinced. Next she asked for guidance in the form of a witchcraft prophetic dream. In her dream the voice clearly said, "Stay put! Your house will sell in April and you need to be there." This time she was convinced, but it was a very nervous April. Nothing happened until the 22nd when they received an offer for an all cash deal subject to closing within two weeks. If they had gone on to Phoenix, they would have lost this deal on the house! Guidance and Prophetic dreams will come to all who are alert in White Witchcraft. Let's begin with a broad look at the whole field of divination.

Forms of Divination

We will consider the divinatory arts in groups related to the degree of psychic development required. The first group appears quite mechanical and involves physical and/or mathematical props. The Witch's Runes, I Ching, Tarot, Palmistry and Astrology fall into this first category.

Next we will view the systems that require an assist from nature—the direction of flight of a bird, bird songs, the course of a spider across a piece of paper, or smoke direction from burning incense all have meaning if you're interested in this form of "future seeing."

The third group is closer to true mediumship. This involves the interpretation of symbols— dreams are a good source of prophetic symbols, but psychics have used patterns in scattered grain, tea leaves, tobacco, splattered eggs or the intestines of a chicken. The last group involves developing a greater degree of mediumship or psychic ability. It includes crystal gazing, trance, precognitive clairvoyance, clairaudience and the like. Don't sell yourself short here, *you* may easily develop any or all of these faculties into a most useful tool. But let's start with the "easy" things first.

HOW YOU CAN PREDICT THE FUTURE
WITH MECHANICAL HELP OR PROPS

In all methods of divination it is the proper setting of the mood that insures your accuracy in foreseeing the future. A comfortable amount of reverence for the ritual or method is necessary—or to put it the other way, a flip question is sure to get a flip answer of its own kind.

One good method of getting sound advice was imported from witchcraft into many a Christian Endeavor group. Have you tried the following or at least heard a friend say, "When I'm seeking the answer to a big problem, I ask for guidance and then open my Bible at random. With my eyes closed, I put my finger on a passage. It almost always gives me the best possible solution." This is an adaptation of the broad method called *Rhapsodomancy*. The source of your guidance can be a dictionary, thesaurus, Bhagavad Gita, Bible, or your favorite reference book. The best technique is to write your question first—the process of organizing your thoughts well enough to communicate them in writing helps to sweep away the confusion that would otherwise block your clear answer, and it helps you to interpret when the answer seems a bit vague. Then sit quietly with your eyes closed and ask the question aloud of your own higher nature or your spirit forces.

With the eyes still closed, tumble the book around in your hands until you are sure that you don't know which end is up. Open it or let it fall open, and put your finger somewhere on a page. (A more sophisticated approach is to run your finger along the page until you seem to feel a warm spot.) Open your eyes and read your message in the passage beneath your finger.

HOW OTTO Z. USED A DICTIONARY
FOR A FINANCIAL PROBLEM

Otto Z. had been offered a chance to invest in a new restaurant franchise. He was quite enthusiastic, but since it required risking his entire life savings plus going heavily into debt, he decided to seek a peek into the future. Not being very religious by inclination, Otto decided to use his dictionary for the source of guidance. He followed the tumbling procedure and found under his finger the definition of the word *swindle*. This prompted him to seek detailed information on the firm from his banker and on the strength of his growing doubts he postponed his investment. In less than six months, the firm was in bankruptcy. Otto has thanked his dictionary many times.

The explanation for such things was given by the great psychiatrist C.G. Jung when he coined the term *synchronicity*. When it is an idea's time to manifest, it seeks as many avenues as are available to it. Certainly it is always time for the truth to manifest. Let's explore other methods of letting through the truth of your future.

How to Make and Use Your Own Atlantean Witch's Runes

A fascinating method of predicting the future is the use of witch's runes. Runes are small sticks with dots or symbols. There are many different sets of symbols, but the general use is the same with all. The origin of the runes is obscured by history, as is so much of witchcraft lore. In our past life regression research at E.S.P. Laboratory, we encountered a set of runes in the ancient (mythical as far as modern science is concerned) civilization of Atlantis. We updated the symbology according to our best understanding and made up a few experimental sets for use of selected people around the country. The method is quick and fun—and amazingly accurate for many. They are simple to make, and you would like a set of your own. So we will explain how to make your runes before we talk about how to use them.

You will need twelve flat sticks ("popsicle sticks" or wood tongued depressors will do, although the ancient art would require that you make them yourself from a willow branch). Each side of each stick (or rune) will be inscribed with a different symbol. You artistically inclined witches can draw or paint beautiful pictures on your runes, but the written word will do as well. Each rune will have a positive symbol on one side and a negative one on the other. Understand that the work negative in this use represents polarity and is not necessarily "bad." Inscribe your runes as follows:

Rune # 1:   Positive side— Flowers, symbolizing beauty, loveliness and appreciation.

             Negative side— Weeds, symbolizing that which limits and depreciates beauty.

Rune # 2:   Positive side— A Dollar Bill, symbolizing abundance and material riches.

             Negative side— A Penny Flying Away, symbolizing material lack and the inability to attract riches.

Rune # 3:   Positive side— A Heart, symbolizing human love, warmth and goodness.

             Negative side— A Rain Cloud, symbolizing the cold and dark side of human nature.

Rune # 4:   Positive side— The Sun, symbolizing the life giving power and the love of the Infinite, and active spiritual strength.

             Negative side— The Moon, symbolizing passivity and receptiveness. The Sun is the Father principle and the Moon is the Mother principle.

Rune # 5:   Positive side— Jupiter, symbolizing expansion, opulence and easy accomplishment.

             Negative side— Saturn, symbolizing contraction, thrift and exactitude. The great teacher is Saturn while the benefactor is Jupiter.

Rune # 6:   Positive side— Laughter, symbolizing happy fellowship with people.

             Negative side— Loneliness, symbolizing withdrawal from life.

Rune # 7:   Positive side— Friendly Spirit, symbolizing tangible help and loving companionship and care from spirit teachers and friends.

             Negative side— Negative Entity, symbolizing interference from spirits lower on the evolutionary scale.

Rune # 8:   Positive side— Beaver, symbolizing industriousness and good discipline.

             Negative side— Mule, symbolizing the excesses of discipline or complete lack of discipline as characterized by excessive stubborness.

Rune # 9:	Positive side—	Shamrock, symbolizing good luck and the happy attunement with nature spirits and nature herself.
	Negative side—	Black Cat, symbolizing the state of being out of tune that man calls "bad luck."
Rune #10:	Positive side—	Spiritual, symbolizing the generous and loving use of your powers and seeking of spiritual growth.
	Negative side—	Black Magic, symbolizing the inflated ego that mistakenly seeks to play God and control the destinies of others unfairly.
Rune #11:	Positive side—	Lion, symbolizing courage, physical strength and determination.
	Negative side—	Mouse, symbolizing fear, cowardice and weakness.
Rune #12:	Positive side—	Shiva, symbolizing cooperation with the forces of change.
	Negative side—	Rock, symbolizing the resistence to change, stagnation or lack of progress, standstill.

How to Cast Your Witches Runes

Prepare to use your runes by writing the question just as you would for the book tumbling method. Then measure a piece of string one yard long and lay it on the floor in an east/west direction. Stand a foot or so away from the east end of the string and face east (away from the string). Ask your question aloud while holding the full set of runes in your right hand, then without looking toss them over your left shoulder toward the string with one gentle motion. The pattern of the fallen runes on the floor gives you the answer, there remains only a small matter of interpretation.

The time factor of your answer starts a foot or so in front (east) of the string. That area represents the distant past. The first foot of string is the immediate past, the middle foot the present, the far part of the string is the immediate future and the area past the west end of the string is the distant future. Proximity to the ribbon indicates the importance of the power symbolized by each rune, and the angle tells you the relative power of the influence—perpendicular to the string being the strongest and most sudden, parrallel the weakest but longest acting, and the angles in between making the shading. To interpret your answer, let the *feeling* of the interaction of the forces give you sound and useful advice. Yes or no questions are answered by the runes with a degree of probability—but isn't this like a weather forecast, say a 90 percent probability of rain?

Practical Use of Witches Runes

Do the runes work? I have found them extremely useful for myself, but you could easily say that I'm prejudiced. Let's look at a report from F.S.: "Those Atlantean Runes are completely uncanny! Yesterday I asked them if I should let my 17-year-old daughter remain in northern California for her last year of school rather than force her to come back to Los Angeles. Only one rune landed near the string. It was exactly perpendicular and right in the middle. It was *spiritual.* Today I received a letter from my daughter stating a strong plea that her spiritual growth would be greatly helped by staying up north. I already had my answer from the runes."

The I Ching or Chinese Book of the Changes, Tarot, Palmistry, Numerology and Astrology belong in this section, but each would require a book in itself. We will simply suggest that you put these subjects on your list for personal investigation when you feel the time is right.

How to Predict the Future with an Assist from Nature

The direction of flight of a bird, the course taken by a spider or ladybug, the action of smoke rising from incense or gyrations of a candle flame have all been successfully used as methods of predicting the future by people who feel a rapport with natural things through witchcraft. You will find nature quite cooperative if you are sincere and enjoy rapport with her creatures. The birds, insects and other "lower forms of life" are in better tune with the forces of change than the average human being, so we can see some rationale for their future seeing ability. Is it beneath your dignity to ask a spider for help with your problem? If so, just ignore this short section. As for me, I've learned to accept help and valid information from any source that has proved itself reliable—and you can't test reliability without asking questions!

The trick in witchcraft is to tell your instrumentality (bird, spider, ladybug, etc.) what action you will expect for a "yes" and for a "no" answer. In the beginning you may prefer incense or a candle because such materials will stay where you put them until you are ready to use them. There are standard ways of working with a candle, for instance. In the old witchcraft tradition a brand new candle may be used to answer one question. You simply ask your question aloud of the candle, then light it. If the flame goes way up in a few seconds, the answer is "yes"; but if it shrinks very low, the answer is "no." That way is fine for amateurs, but it wastes a lot of candles at best.

A Special Candle Usage

Let's examine a more sophisticated use of the same basic idea as reported to us by Dorothy C: "I have developed a wonderful rapport with the candle on my altar. I thought I felt it reaching out to me one night, so I talked to it. I told it I would like to be friends and asked if it would answer me. I suggested that its flame lean toward me for "yes," away from me for "no," and sidewise if it couldn't answer. Very quickly the flame leaned way over towards me and I felt an emanation or glow that I could only describe as friendship. Next I asked it to show me how it would say "no," and it quickly leaned directly away from me. When I asked if it could tell me of the future, the flame leaned toward me again in a most friendly manner. For several months now it has been my personal investment counselor. It has accurately predicted the direction of movement of my stocks on a weekly basis—and I credit it for my being several thousand dollars richer. When the first candle burned away, its replacement was as friendly. I wouldn't trade my candles for the best investment banker in the country."

The same principle can be applied to the fumes from burning incense or to any of the small household insects—if you trade your killer instinct for friendship and compassion for them. Common sense will keep you from acting on the advice of your small insect friends until you have proved its validity to yourself. But again let's comment that you can't prove it without asking a few intelligent questions.

How to Be Your Own Witchcraft Medium Through Symbol Interpretation

"Future-seeing" help from bugs and candles makes good sense as a logical combination of synchronicity and your love affair with life. Our next methods are an extension of your love affair with the "little people." The free flowing mind that enjoys regular interchange with the nature spirits can easily read clues to future events from the suggestions of pictures and symbols. Where shall we find the pictures and symbols? And how shall *you* interpret them?

Methods of acquiring prophetic symbology abound in all occult and witchcraft lore. Basically it is harnessing the powerful faculty of child like imagination—the power that could look up at the clouds when you were a child and see elephants, giraffes, ships, clowns, palaces and a whole world of adventure right up in your own piece of sky. This happy imagination is a pre-logic faculty that can bring you insights into now and the future with uncanny accuracy, but only if you use it as a tool in the proper sequence of planned program. Let's give a step by step approach right here:

Step 1. Write your question or request for insight. The process of organizing your thoughts well enough to write them on a piece of paper focuses your subconscious mechanisms and helps put them in tune with the nature spirits who will help you.

Step 2. Use all or your favorite parts of the nature spirit invocation ritual, and invite their friendly participation. This is much like setting the mood before you ask for information from a knowledgeable friend in a physical body. Make it pleasant for your friends so that they will enjoy sharing their *accurate* information.

Step 3. Perform the required physical act. Here you swirl the tea leaves, sprinkle the sand, toss the breadcrumbs, or blow out the contents of the egg. (We will touch the individual methods at the end of this section.)

Step 4. In the "little child" state of mind, note the symbols without pausing to consider their meaning. This is the purely "imaginative" part of the operation and it is a major secret of success. If you stop to interpret the symbols at this point, you will get too intellectually and emotionally involved and so cut off the source of information before you get the whole story. Simply note the flow of symbolic pictures and the order in which they present themselves to you. I encourage my students to write down key words to describe the symbols here before there is any attempt at interpretation.

Step 5. Interpret the symbols according to their logical meaning to you and the way they seem to make you feel. If this process begins to generate anxiety, then set your notes aside and come back to them when you have rebuilt the relaxed and detached state. Anxiety during Step 4 will cut off the flow of symbology, but anxiety here in Step 5 will cause misinterpretation of the message.

Let's examine the mechanics of a few variations of Step 3:

Tea Leaf Reading is a very popular method. Naturally this requires brewing a cup of tea with loose tea (a tea bag or tea ball won't work). Your favorite brand or mixture of teas is fine for this. When the liquid is nearly consumed, invite your nature spirit participation as you swirl the leaves around so that some stick to the sides of the cup. They can then be "read" in place, or some practitioners turn the cup upside down and read the patterns that fall into the saucer.

Sand Reading can be traced to ancient Egypt, and **Bread Crumb Reading** is mentioned in the Talmud. The techniques are the same for these. A pie tin or cookie sheet is used to catch the sand or crumbs. When you feel in tune with your nature spirit help, slowly sprinkle a big handful into the receptacle and watch for symbols and patterns as the sand or crumbs fall.

Egg Reading may seem a bit more like a gimmick but history records the use of chicken entrails and many other "exotic" props for the same purpose. Again, a pie tin or cookie sheet is a good idea to keep from making a big mess. Using a needle or pin, put a hole in each end of a raw egg. Call in your nature spirits, then blow into one end of the egg, thus forcing the material out the other end. There is much symbology to be seen in the patterns it makes on the pie tin.

Symbol interpretation itself has been the subject of many scholarly books. But you can make it both simple and accurate with a little practice. There are supposedly universal meanings to some symbols, but trying to use them as a rote code will generally miss the mark. The test is simple, what does the symbol mean to *you?* By keeping a notebook in which you record your questions and the symbols that came in answer, you will very shortly learn the language of your own subconscious mind. Then you have a powerful tool for glimpsing the future—and many other things that we will unfold as the chapters continue.

How a "Long Shot" at the Horse Races
Paid Off Through Witchcraft

R.R. was planning a trip to the races on Saturday. Friday evening she asked for a tip from her nature spirit friends. This was her report: "I tried to think of a method, and remembered that I had some breadcrumbs in the house. So I got out a cookie sheet and the breadcrumbs and had a little ritual. I used my prosperity oil and lit a prosperity incense. Then I chanted and asked my friends for the tip. The crumb patterns I had strewn seemed to show a heart with an arrow in it and then a bow. Sure enough, there in the ninth race was a horse called Cupid's Bow. Playing on my own during the day I was about $40 behind when the ninth race came up, and Cupid's Bow was a long shot, about 20 to 1. I took a deep breath and bought a $10 win ticket. I had lots of nice things to say to my nature spirit friends when I finished the day better than $150 ahead"!

There are as many uses for these techniques as there are people. Try it and find fresh help for getting ahead in life.

HOW TO BE YOUR OWN WITCHCRAFT MEDIUM

When you mention Witchcraft, a common vision conjured up is a long-nosed, wrinkled-faced old hag dressed in flowing black with a pointed hat stirring a steaming cauldrom. That's a bunch of nonsense of course, but the secondary vision of a person seeing visions in a crystal ball has greater validity. When you have learned to see pictures and symbols in tea leaves and breadcrumbs the bridge to the purer forms of mediumship is well established. A bowl of water will serve you quite as well as the traditional crystal ball, and you will finally graduate to seeing the whole bit on the little television screen inside your head. The same five steps we used in our last section apply to crystal gazing (or shall we call it water gazing?). Let's call this part a discussion of Step 3.

THE SECRET OF GETTING PICTURES IN A CRYSTAL

There is a visual trick to getting pictures in a crystal ball or bowl of water. We assume you will try the water first since it is more readily available and much cheaper. It is within the realm of your *peripheral vision* that all manner of pictorial symbology is available. After the nature spirit attunement, the trick is to focus your normal front vision on the *bottom* of the bowl. Then with the peripheral vision you can observe the symbols as they appear on the water's surface. We all have peripheral vision—that's what defends the sides of your car while you are driving. You can be looking straight at the road ahead, when your attention is diverted by a movement far to one side. The difference between water gazing and driving is that you do not shift the focus of your eyes to get the pictures. When the side vision suggests danger to the car, it is prudent and natural to take a direct look in preparation for evasive action. But in water gazing, this would focus away your pictures. Resist the impulse to refocus your gaze to the surface, and you can keep your pictures as long as you like. Practice will make you very good at this, but you will need to keep your notes and study symbol interpretation in this also.

Hints for Interpreting Symbology

I'd like to refer you to my book, *Helping Yourself with ESP*, for more background; but let's look for a moment at your growing faculty of precognitive clairvoyance. When you are accustomed to producing pictures on the surface of your bowl of water, it is a short step to close you eyes and look for similar pictures and symbology on the TV screen inside your head. I can't imagine shutting my eyes and seeing only darkness! There is always a flow of energy and light patterns—colors may progress from one side of your head to the other, or you may seem to be looking at swirling cloud formations. And occasionally, you will see a complete picture in 3-D living color. Your growing ability to recognize and interpret symbols can be applied here with fantastic results. One nice thing about this method is that you need no props. Your head is always with you.

Your nature spirit friends often use a sense of humor to bring you useful messages. A legal secretary came to me for help in interpreting a symbol. There was a very sticky human relations situation involving a young attorney at her office and she had asked for advice. On the TV screen inside her head had come just one symbol, a great big sloppy bird struggling to get off the ground. I teased her with the comment, "They are obviously telling you to relax and play it like a big sloppy bird. When an albatross is in flight it appears graceful and magnificent. Nobody remembers the ridiculous scene of its struggle to get airborne. Take it to heart and win." By relaxing she was able to find the confidence and humorous insight to turn a sticky situation into a nice place to work. So can you!

CHAPTER POINTS TO REMEMBER

1) A very natural desire of all human beings is the ability to see into the future. By applying a few simple witchcraft techniques, you can develop your future seeing ability to degrees you have not dared dream possible.

2) Future seeing is called *Divination* or *Divine Revelation*. You are in the company of such greats as Plato and Socrates when you work to unfold your Witchcraft arts of future seeing.

3) There are elementary techniques of Witchcraft divination that require no "mediumistic ability." Using them will help you to unfold the more sophisticated methods that do use your natural mediumship. Rhapsodomancy and the Runes are very good methods for beginners. Develop your accuracy with these simple techniques and use it as a springboard to ever greater future seeing ability.

4) Gaining a rapport with your candle flame can lead to many useful contacts with insects and nature spirits as sound advisors on the future.

5) Practice the 5 step method of future seeing through the symbols of tea leaves, sand, breadcrumbs or the egg method. This is the gateway to true mediumship.

6) Your personal pure mediumship can come easily from water gazing or just paying attention to the symbols on the TV screen inside your head. It will greatly enrich your life to allow these hidden talents fresh expression in your daily activities.

Chapter Six

How to Use Rituals and Spells
to Attract and Hold a Lover

*L*et's start this chapter with a most important exercise for attracting love. Too often people think of witchcraft just in terms of compelling love potions, or the man who, when his girl spurns him says, "Now I'm going to cast a spell and make her come crawling back begging that I take her love." But that would be a terrible way to live! Who wants a puppet for a lover?

Instead, let's work to build a very special and strong consciousness. When you have it and walk in it, *you will never want for love.* The idea is to make every moment—and this includes the times when you are asleep—*every moment of your life will become a happy love affair.* We will work to make every thing you think or do part of a love affair with love itself, and let it shape your life with an exciting new approach to all things. Then success, love and happiness are yours! And you can keep them forever with Witchcraft help.

How shall you begin this important exercise? This is a morning ritual that begins by waking up with a smile. The complete exercise is designed to be used for one week, but if you do it well, parts of it will be etched into your being and you will continue them forever. We seek to build a new loving outlook on life deep into your inner consciousness. At first you may need a big sign by the bed to remind you to wake up with a smile, but it's worth it. Before you get up, generate a feeling of thanksgiving to your own highest concept of God for the simple beauty of life and the opportunity to bound out of bed into the gorgeous new day—even if you are going to work!

Next comes the ritual of preparing your body for the new day. At least for the one week of the exercise, prepare it as if you were getting ready for a special date with your greatest love. Use your most provocative shaving lotions or perfume and get all spruced up so that you have the confidence of a well-groomed feeling. Make each little step of the grooming a part of getting ready to *enjoy!* This is a special part of the ritual of really loving life—each tiny step is happy and beautiful.

How to Condition Your Aura

Before you think of leaving the dressing area, it is time to clean and perfume your aura the same way you did your body. (Auras were discussed in a previous chapter.) Stop for a brief 30 seconds to 30 minutes, depending on you. How long does it take for *you* to feel that your aura is as clean as the body you have freshened and the lovely clothes you have put on it? I use a simple technique of asking for Light to bathe me and cleanse my aura. Feel a powerful shaft of Light beaming down and washing your aura just as a running brook would wash your body. Then send the Light before you. Direct it mentally as you say aloud: "I send the Light before me to make the path easy and the way straight. It brings inspiration, upliftment, effectiveness, enthusiam and joy to every being who comes close to my aura. I am Light going to meet Light, and only GOOD can result."

How to Intensify the Love Ritual

Now how about breakfast? Do you appreciate the *Love* in the preparation? If you fix your own breakfast it's all the more important to put extra love in the cooking. All day, pause before you start each meal or snack—enjoy the love in the food, both the loving service in its preparation and the love of the Infinite that makes food available to you at all. Feel a stream of ever increasing opulence, love and joy being rained down upon you from the Infinite and *respond* to it. Strive to make every moment of each 24 hours a *ritual of love* for the one week. Be completely conscious of love in all its forms, and let the week of feasting in this manner leave you changed for the better forever. Then we can parlay the new love consciousness into the fulfillment of your happiest dreams.

Practical Benefits from Love Ritual

Does the exercise sound a bit "hokey"? Don't let that discourage you. Our research reports from this are full of enthusiam and excitement. Here's a typical comment: "I have lived alone for ten years now. It has been a dull, lonely life from my empty apartment to my dull job and back. Nobody ever even called me on the phone. I decided that at least I have plenty of time to try your week's love ritual, so I did. By the third day, people at the office who had never noticed me were coming up to chat and invite me to lunch. I have made ten wonderful new friends in just one week, and one of them looks like a real love interest! It's unbelievable after the years of loneliness. I should have tried something like this years ago"!

Love Spells Belong to the Moon, Venus, Diana, Hecate, Aphrodite and Ishtar

Spend the week to build your fresh love consciousness. Your love potions and spells will fall on rock if you are still harboring a rejection complex—prepare the fertile soil of love for your happy planting. Particularly if you have a specific person in mind, you will need the power of the love consciousness to reach out and attract. But let's take care that we avoid the pitfalls of black magic—to control an individual is to usurp his or her freedom of choice, and that in the modern vernacular "plays hell with your karma." To interest, intrigue, excite and entice is perfectly fair game, but to control sets up forces that we can all do better without. Let's leave it this way: you wouldn't want to surrender control of your life to someone else, so don't leave yourself open to attack by trying to control another.

EFFECTIVE LOVE INVOCATIONS AND SKILLS

All good love spells somehow court the favor of the ancient gods and goddesses. When this is combined with help from the nature spirits, you will find your work irresistible. Our purpose here is to give a few sample love spells to get you familiar with the idea. Then you can combine them or add your own personality, preferably in simple rhyme to tap the age old powers of love. The approach is a natural one—love seeks its own fulfillment and you have only to help it a little bit to let it find that fulfillment through you. As you work with the chants, repeating them often, you will feel a special affinity to one or two of the love deities of old—and indeed you will feel the presence and power of your special ones a constant source of comfort and help. Use the following chants to help you get the feel of the work:

INVOCATION OF VENUS

When Rome ruled all the world, 'tis said,
    Dear Venus, hearts of men you led
To love, the great delight of life
    With spell of beauty, not of strife.
Your power's still undimmed, I know,
    To me true love in life now show.
Bring love to me on wings of sound,
    Let happiness and joy abound.
With every act and thought of mine,
    Let me attract my love divine.
Now quickly bring my love to me,
    And as my will, so mote it be!

SPELL FOR IMPATIENT LOVERS

Lovely Shiva, Agni, Thor,
    Fix it so we wait no more.
Sweep the problems out to sea,
    Build things like they ought to be
Light and love, eternal bliss,
    Give it as your loving kiss.
Happiness for all we pray,
    Help us turn the night to day.
Bringing hope and help to all,
    In answer to our fervent call.
I thank you now and *feel* your love,
    The answer's coming from above.

POWERFUL LOVE SPELL

Ishtar, Isis, hear my cry.
    Without true love, my soul shall die.
Aphrodite, come to me,
    And bring the one I ache to see.
Freya, Cupid, Eros, hear
    This call I send you loud and clear.
Thor and Agni, Mighty Zeus,

This word to you is for good use.
Bring a love that's good and bold,
        I charge you, mighty Gods of old.
My true love must come now to me,
        And as my will so mote it be!

A Factual Case History

Do the incantations work? Here's a typical case: A couple in a metaphysical class. She was divorced and raising her two teenage children. There was work, care for the kids, and an occasional occult or religious class—she was lonely. He was married, but equally lonely. His wife seemed to have withdrawn into herself, so for him it had become work, work, and an occasional metaphysical class. It was natural for two lonely people to stop for coffee after class, and they quickly discovered many interests and tastes in common. What had started as a casual friendship soon ripened into a deep love. It came as a surprise to both of them. Bill had been completely honest, so Sally knew he was married. When Bill finally gulped and said, "I love you, Sally," they agreed that they had a big problem. As Bill put it, "My wife doesn't work or anything. All she wants to do is just sit there watching television or reading. She certainly wouldn't agree to a divorce." But Sally and Bill were budding Witchcraft students, concerned with possible old karmic problems as well as the current mess. So they decided to put off any action for 60 days while they used the "Spell for Impatient Lovers." I have prescribed it for six couples who have come to me with circumstances like those of Bill and Sally. All six couples are now happily married to each other. The shortest time it took to get results was 10 days—the longest time was 92 days. I have also suggested the chant for just one party to a similar situation on three occasions. In all three of these cases there was no result, but I feel that the 100 percent identical results in the two different type cases is highly evidential. The power of two people working in agreement on a truly common cause is a lot greater than two people working independently.

But what if you don't have a partner to work with? Practice the other chants in this section, or change one to make it feel just right for you. Then blend it into the full scale love attracting ritual at the end of this chapter.

How to Build a Love Attracting Thoughtform

Love potions and techniques enter into the practical aspects of all forms of human relations. Anything that improves your appearance or enhances the impression you make can properly be termed a tool of Witchcraft. The odor of your perfume or shaving lotion combines with the colors of your clothing to add a special something to the magnetic force that is you. We will talk about exotic love potions in a moment, they are tools of the trade, but we need a naturally alluring *you* to use the tools effectively. Let's begin by suggesting an addition to your week's *love affair with love* exercise. Practice being exciting. Try using a bit of extra eye contact. There is a real Witchcraft energy that flows from your eyes. A little thought will prove that to you. How many times have you stared at the back of someone's head and watched them turn around to see who was looking at them? And *you* have reacted to others also.

You can also send feelings of warmth and friendship along the beam of energy that flows from your eyes. It's only necessary to *will* that it flow. Add to that the power of the breath and the tingle of a special touch in Witchcraft and you will find yourself suddenly extremely desirable to someone you want to impress. You can excite almost any member of the opposite sex by artfully contriving to breathe on the neck of the area behind an ear as you gently touch it with your lips. As you practice the art of being naturally exciting, and regularly exercise your sense of humor, you are preparing for the special joys of sharing a personal relationship.

Now that you are primed for the "infighting," let's talk about interesting a particular or special individual. Again I am careful to use the word *interest* as opposed to *control*, because we don't want to drag the person to you kicking and screaming. Let's settle for ideas like intrigue, pique, excite, interest, fascinate and perhaps "turn on." That is the safe and effective way to use your witchcraft. The first step beyond the normal masculine or feminine wiles is the *thoughtform*. You should be comfortable with the *thoughtform* concept from the work of Chapter 4, so this is a natural for you. With the mood of love set just right, hold your hands out and let the energy flow between them. This is the easiest *thoughtform* you will ever build because it draws from the basic energy of reproduction of the species. As the energy field begins to take form, fill it with the image of your chosen lover and feed it the most blatantly erotic thoughts you can imagine. At this point, some students of the art would suggest self stimulation of your erogenous zones as a way of adding power to the *thought-form*. I prefer not to make a value judgment here, that choice is up to you, but when you feel that your *thoughtform* has been built to a maximum of power, order it to: "Go to my lover and deliver my message. Excite, entice, stimulate and fill my lover's being with thoughts of me."

THE IMPORTANCE OF THE AURA

Next time you fine yourself entertaining erotic thoughts about a seemingly casual acquaintance, examine your aura to see if these thoughts are being sent to you—you just might be missing a happy bet! I have conclusively proved to myself that they were being used on me on more than one occasion, and I have used them myself with very happy success. But don't take my word for it, it works for anybody.

How Mary Got Her Man

Mary was in the stenographic pool of a large company. The young assistant sales manager just didn't seem to notice her. She had tried several new hair styles and the most provocative dresses that propriety would allow, but to no avail. After three fruitless months of no progress, Mary decided to experiment with a love *thoughtform* based on her classes in my group. It was easy to put his image in it because it was clearly etched in her mind. And it took only a mild amount of imagination to feel him caressing her and kissing her passionately. The *thoughtform* seemed to literally soak up the erotic feelings she generated and quickly became a very vital, living entity. Upon her firmly spoken order, it happily left to carry out its mission. The very next afternoon he discreetly asked her for a date. It was a storybook romance from the start, with response building response—all the way to a lovely wedding and three wonderful children. It can work for *you,* too. But give your *thoughtforms* more than one day to work, sometimes he or she is preoccupied so it may take a week or two to get your lover's attention. But perseverance will win!

QUESTIONS AND ANSWERS ABOUT THOUGHTFORMS

Here the typical student's question is: Is the *thoughtform* received at exactly the same time is sent? The answer is: not necessarily. This is the difference between telepathic communication and *thoughtforms*. In telepathy your subject must be receptive at the time you are sending the message if it is to be received, but a *thoughtform* is more like a Western Union boy who is ordered to go out and deliver your message. The order is to deliver it, and if the addressee is not home or not receptive, wait until he (or she) is home and receptive, and then deliver it.

Another very pertinent question is: Do these *thoughtforms* ever backfire? Here an illustration of the danger may help. It was the second marriage for each and had been a comfortable six years, but Jim felt that the zest was gone from their sex life. He had tactfully suggested trying some tentative wife swapping in hopes of awakening Margie's desires once more, but she had reacted with horror at the idea. The level of frustration was building up for Jim so he decided to work on a wife swapping *thoughtform* anyway. He had mentally picked out another couple about their same ages. Jim's basic approach was somewhat sloppy—the feeling was, "If this only works half way, let's be sure it at least gets me into Josie's good graces for anything I want!"

Jim kept up his *thoughtform* building work every night for three weeks, and he was enjoying the prospect more and more— even thinking of performing in a sexy way with Josie while the other two merely watched approvingly. In the middle of the fourth week came the backfire! It was Saturday afternoon, Jim was watching a football game on TV while Margie was cleaning in the kitchen. Jim answered the doorbell and was confronted by a short, "seedy looking" unkempt young man whose opening statement was: "Hi. I find myself sexually attracted to your wife. I would gladly practice wife swapping with you, but my lovely wife is visiting her mother. Meanwhile, I must have your wife, now." Jim's childhood "Victorian" values suddenly snapped into play, and he almost threw the young man down a flight of stairs as he cursed and threatened to call the police. Jim says he has never told this to anyone but me. He quickly and quietly went back to his altar and reprogrammed the *thoughtform* for peace, love and protection—the young stranger was never seen in the neighborhood again. Jim says, "He must have crawled right back under the rock my sloppy *thoughtform* had lifted for him"!

Similarly, your romantic *thoughtforms* aimed at a specific person, may generate a few extraneous invitations. I have always considered them flattering, and it is easy to give a polite, "No thank you," with a friendly smile. It's only when you are skirting areas of potential guilt or some emotional hang-up that there can be negative fallout from your work.

How to Make an Effective Love Potion

Let's turn our attention to a more tangible love potion before we put it all together in the complete love attracting ritual. In Chapter 3 we presented a good formula for love attracting powder. It is best used as a sachet—one carried somewhere on the person, and another stored in the dresser with your fancy underwear. Like the love perfumed oils, this is to build excitement into your aura. Follow through with the odors in all that you do. The best choice of shaving lotion or perfume is the one that smells "sexiest" to *you.* For the complete ritual we will begin in a moment, assemble your love attracting powder, love oils or perfume, love attracting incense—along with the normal candles (red is good here), the jar of earth, salt water, and your chalice filled with love potion wine.

We now have only to give you the recipe for the love potion wine, and the ritual can begin. Consecrate a cool, dark place for storage of a pint bottle. Then to a pint of your favorite dry red wine add a teaspoon of juniper berries and 1/4 teaspoon of basil. Put the bottle in the prepared place and chant over it three times:

> "Venus, Cupid, Eros, friends
>   Your help will serve my rightful ends.
> My loving trust appeals to thee,
>   Please send my true love straight to me."

Each night for seven straight days, repeat the chant over your bottle three or more times. Then remove it and strain it while repeating the chant three more times. Use one third of the liquid in your ritual each night for three nights. This love potion is also wonderful when shared with your chosen lover—but don't use it unless you are serious!

A Complete Love Attracting Ritual

Since this is our first presentation of a full/special ritual we will give it in its complete form with all the chants in one place for future reference. In later chapters we will suggest modifications for other special purposes. Before you begin, be sure that you have assembled all the materials you will need. Nothing will blow the power of your ritual so completely as reaching for the next goodie and realizing that you forgot to bring it with you to the Witches's altar. Next, prepare yourself as if you were getting ready for the most important date of your life. Take a long, luxurious shower or bath, do a nice job on your hair, and use your sexiest cologne or shaving lotion very liberally. Take the telephone off the hook on the way, and lock or otherwise be sure that your altar area is safe from interruption.

For a special ritual such as this, I always go to my altar completely nude, but if a pair of panties or shorts will make you more comfortable, we can compromise that far. Smile at the face in your altar mirror, and begin by setting your protection of Light. Mentally picture a sphere of bright white Light surrounding you as you chant:

> "Rama, Agni, send the Light to me.
>   Rama, Agni, send the powerful Light to me.
> Sweep away the things that harm
>   Let them cause me no alarm.
> Rama, Agni, send the Light that sets me free."

Use each of the chants at least three times as you work for the *feeling* of tremendous power. Next sprinkle your salt water liberally around the altar area as you chant:

> "Salt and water, power to thee.
>   No spell nor unknown purpose be
> Not in complete accord with me.
>   And as my will, so mote it be."

Then comes the ritual lighting of your red candles and love

incense. Strike your match, and light the candles, starting with the one on your right. Light the incense from a candle and chant:

> "Creatures of fire, this charge I give,
>   No evil in my presence live,
> No phantom, spook, nor spell my stay
>   Around this place, not night nor day.
> Hear my will addressed to thee.
>   And as my work, so mote it be"!

Now anoint your brow, heart, and genital with your favorite love oil, and chant:

> "And now this oily essence fair
>   Adds its great power to the air,
> Attracting spirits of the Light
>   Bringing love both day and night.
> This charge is true and proper, see,
>   And as my will, so mote it be."

Next, fill one or two sachet bags with fresh love drawing powder and sprinkle a bit of loose powder on your altar as you chant:

> "Sachet of love, with power filled
>   Bring soon my love as I have willed.
> Magnetic aura make for me,
>   And as my word, so mote it be"!

Now we have reached the point of *thoughtform* building. Hold your hands out and *will* the energy to flow between them. Here we can choose our chant—the Invocation of Venus or the Spell for Impatient Lovers, depending on the situation for which you are performing the ritual. While you feel the energy flow building between your hands, chant—(Here I have assumed the Venus chant):

> "When Rome ruled all the world, 'tis said,
>   Dear Venus, hearts of men you led
> To love, the great delight of life
>   With spell of beauty, not of knife.
> Your power's still undimmed, I know,
>   To me true love in life now show.

Bring love to me on wings of sound,
 Let happiness and joy abound.
With every act and thought of mine,
 Let me attract my love divine.
Now quickly bring my love to me,
 And as my will, so mote it be"!

When you know the *thoughtform* is well built, it's time for the celebration. Pick up your chalice of love potion wine and toast your *thoughtform* and the image in your mirror. Take a comfortable sip and chant:

"Ishtar, Isis, hear my cry.
 Without true love my soul shall die.
Aphrodite, come to me,
 And bring the one I ache to see.
Freya, Cupid, Eros, hear
 This call I send you loud and clear,
Thor and Agni, Mighty Zeus,
 This word to you is for good use.
Bring a love that's good and bold,
 I charge you, mighty Gods of old.
My true love must come now to me,
 And as my will, so mote it be"!

Continue to toast and chant until the wine is all consumed. Then wrap up your ritual with loving thanks. Say: "I give my heartfelt thanks to all the spirits and elementals who have participated here and who continue to help me always. To all elementals who are here, I dismiss you in love. Go in peace to perform your appointed tasks then return to your native habitats, harming no one on the way. Again my loving thanks to all for your help and love. Blessed be."

The Case of Irene R.

My files are full of happy feedback from people who have put their whole being into the spirit of the ritual. Let's share a typical one from Irene R. "That love ritual is the greatest! I enjoyed it in a spirit of both love and power. I used the ritual for the three days, and on the morning of the fourth day, I was transferred to a different department to fill a secretarial opening. The $25 per month raise was nice, but I only kept the job for three weeks. Then I married my boss! He's a dreamboat and we are deliriously happy. Thanks for your part in sending me the ritual—and you can be sure that I thank my nature spirit friends many times each day"!

CHAPTER POINTS TO REMEMBER

1) The one week exercise to build a love affair with love will enrich all parts of your life. Give it a good try.

2) The sample love spells given here have worked for many, but it is always good policy to change and adapt them to suit your special personality.

3) Love attracting *thoughtforms* are the easiest to build. Make yours provocative, exciting and alluring. They can get attention where all your direct approaches have failed.

4) There is no danger from building love attracting *thoughtforms* unless you are treading beyond the limits of your own moral code. The simple caution of being true to your nature is all that you need for safety.

5) Make a checklist of the items you will need for your ritual and be sure you have them all in readiness on or near your altar before you start a ceremony.

6) The love potion wine adds a good deal of power to your ritual. Take the time to prepare it ritually for greatest effect.

7) The complete love attracting ritual is as powerful as the spirit that you put into it. Use it to bring love in spite of all obstacles.

Chapter Seven

How to Use Rituals and Spells to Attract Money and Prosperity

*T*here are many better ways to make money than an 8 to 5 o'clock job—in fact, you never heard of a millionaire who got there by saving it all out of his wages. What the world calls the "lucky break" figures prominently in every success story, but the truth is that breaks are made, they don't just happen. And Witchcraft figures prominently in more "lucky breaks" than you realize. But let's not be ridiculous about it—if you are an office boy with office boy capabilities, Witchcraft may get you promoted to the presidency tomorrow morning, but your lack of ability will get you fired again in less than a month.

Let's use our ritual work to get ahead intelligently—it's all right to get the winners of a few horse races, but when there's executive talent required let's settle for one promotion at a time. Suit each ritual to your present level of capability to assure that you can keep the fruits of your success and grow on to ever greater accomplishment.

HOW TO BUILD YOUR LOVE AFFAIR WITH THE NATURE SPIRITS OF PROSPERITY

The real secret of Witchcraft power lies in the running love affair with the forces of nature. When you are sharing love with the nature spirits, "good luck" follows you everywhere. Your unseen friends delight in showering you with gifts of money that take the form of happy windfalls and prosperous business dealings. Let's be about our business of establishing that love affair. In Chapter 4 we began our work of making friends with the nature spirits, but the *Nature Spirit Invocation* chant and ritual we suggested there was just the get-acquainted phase. Now let's get down to the serious business of convincing your new unseen spirit friends that their growing regard for you should include showering you with plain old-fashioned money. We will give you an addition to the nature spirit ritual, but always keep in mind that you must prove the reality of your love affair with them on a 24-hour, seven-day-week basis if you expect to maintain the happy relationship that keeps financial good fortune smiling on you. Begin your ritual with the normal preparation and invocation of nature spirits as we did in Chapter 4. After three uses of the Nature Spirit Invocation Chant, anoint your brow and heart with Frankessence and Myrrh oils, and bring the power of Jupiter into the ritual with the:

PROSPERITY CHANT

Oh, great and mighty Jupiter, your friendship I do seek.
　　Your emissaries send to me, spirits rich and sleek.
Good nature spirits sent by Jove, your comradeship I love.
　　For bounty and good fellowship my thanks are sent above.
Spirits great, your riches share in fun and friendship true,
　　Prosperity descends on me, my thanks to lovely you.
And now my Light is shining bright, rich green for all to see.
　　Good fortune is my law of life. With thanks, so mote it be.

As always, if you're not comfortable with some part of the chant, adjust it to fit your personality—this one was brought to us from the early days of Rome, and it has worked very well in this century also.

How a Prosperity Chant Worked for W.G.

This is a typical research report. It comes from W.G. in Ohio: "I used the Prosperity Chant at the end of my Nature Spirit Friendship ritual for three straight evenings. The morning of the fourth day I received a call from my insurance broker telling me that he had a check for $950 for me. It has something to do with my life insurance. I don't really understand it yet, but the substance is that yesterday it was worth nothing, and today it brought me $950. That chant is great"! But there are lots of other useful tools, let's look at them.

Money Drawing Washes: How to Increase Your Business

Business a little slow? Would you like to pick it up? Here's a wash recipe that works wonders. Mix an ounce of powdered squill root, an ounce of powdered yellow dock, a teaspoon of cinnamon and tablespoon of salt. Mix it well then add two teaspoons of the mixture to a pint of fresh water. Shake well and store it in a dark place for three full days. When you put it in place, and once each evening while it steeps, chant over your mixture:

BUSINESS IMPROVEMENT CHANT

Nature spirits of the air,
  Bring me business and to spare
Bring me many customers,
  Manly hims and lovely hers.
I serve them well as you do see,
  So this request is right for thee.
Bring them quickly now to me,
  And as my will, so mote it be.

If your business brings in orders and/or checks through the mail, wash your mailbox inside and outside with the mixture each morning, while using the chant. For "walk in" customers, wash down the door handles, the entrance floor and the aisles, while using the chant—and once a week take a turn around the whole building, sprinkling the mixture as you use the chant. Make a fresh batch as often as necessary, but never keep the mixture more than a week after you first use it. This mixture is also good for attracting tenants to an empty apartment. What about results? Again our files are full of happy reports.

Practical Benefits of Prosperity Chants

M.D. of Illinois commented: "The vacancy factor of our building was killing me. Three out of eight apartments had been vacant for almost three months and the financial pressure had me in a state bordering on panic. I was in a hurry to get started so I made two pints of the business improvement herb wash. I only soaked the first batch over night, figuring that I'd do the full three days on the other one, but get going somehow right away. The first morning I washed down the door handles and entrance of my three empty apartments and walked all around the building sprinkling and chanting. In the early afternoon, a couple looked at one apartment and rented it on the spot. 'Not bad, but it could be coincidence,' says I, and when the ritual of the following morning produced no more nibbles I was beginning to really doubt."

"But the next morning, I brought up my big guns, the wash that had enjoyed the full three night chanting ritual. I rented another apartment that night, and the last one in two more days. Since then I have had two other tenants leave, but the wash and chanting have somehow filled the apartments within three days each. It still sounds sort of spooky and superstitious, but you can count me as a believer. As you have often said, 'They pay off on the scoreboard' "!

B.W. owns a small restaurant on the "outskirts of town." After a three-month experiment, she wrote us: "Just at opening time in the morning, I use a tiny mop to wash the floor of the entrance and down the customer side of the counter. This seem to help get the day off to a good start. Then whenever the place gets empty, I lightly mop it down again with the wash—and I swear people come in within five minutes! My accountant says business is up almost 50 percent and it amazes him because times are pretty slow around here. Let's call the 'experiment' an unqualified success."

Money Attracting Powders, Incenses and Perfumes

In Chapter 3 we gave you a formula for a good money-drawing powder and promised the chant that goes with it. Let's start this section with the—

MONEY DRAWING POWDER CHANT

My words have power as of old,
   So hear me now, good Gnomes and Trolls.
Bring me silver, bring me gold,
   Bring the lush green stuff that folds.
Come quickly now, have fun with me,
   And treasure bring most happily.
I speak to you with joy and glee,
   And as my will, so mote it be!

A junior engineer felt discouraged after a year of "no progress" on the job. He had thought of quitting, but the lush days for engineers seemed to be over so to have a job at all was a happy accomplishment. Joe's wife, Clara, was "dabbling in Witchcraft" quite to his amusement. One evening in a joking mood, Joe teased her, "Clara, if that stuff is any good, why don't you cast some sort of a spell to get me a better job"? She answered, "I just happen to have a new recipe for money-drawing powder. Care to help me try it"? So, more as a gag than anything else, Joe chanted with Clara as they ceremonially sprinkled the money-drawing powder into the mailbox. The next day, nothing happened, but Clara teased Joe into joining in the chant again. Still nothing, and it was harder to get Joe to join on the third night, but he did.

The next mail delivery brought a letter from a "Management Consultant Firm" speaking of a job opening and asking for an updated resume. Joe responded and the new job brought almost a $200 per month increase in wages. Although still not thoroughly convinced, Joe has quit pooh-poohing Clara's study of Witchcraft.

SPECIAL AIDS FOR MORE FINANCIAL HELP

Looking for more help? It's readily available. The theory of incense combines ideas of ceremony, sacrifice, mood setting and pleasant odors. Incense comes down to us from the dawn of time as a method of sharing beauty with the nature spirits and the higher spiritual forces. As the physical matter is transmuted on the material levels, it carries the beautiful essences to the higher planes where it attracts and pleases the positive spirits whose help and cooperation we seek.

I use some form of incense at both my morning and evening meditation periods and of course for any special ritual work that I do in between. The response from the unseen side of life should inspire *you* to do likewise. Here is a simple recipe for a good prosperity or money-attracting incense that you can make without a big mess—

Recipe for Prosperity/Money Attracting Incense

7 drams tincture of benzoin	A small pinch of saltpeter
1/2 dram Frankessence (oil)	1/2 dram Myrrh (oil)
1/2 dram Sandalwood oil	1 oz. powdered charcoal

Mix all the liquid ingredients first then add the saltpeter and stir well—this is to insure that there are no concentrations of saltpeter that would make your incense "pop." Then slowly add the charcoal, stirring until you have a mass about the consistency of heavy mud. Spread into a small metal or plastic box, and cut it into cubes when it is nearly dry (about 1/2 hour to 45 minutes after you spread it). You'll find that it helps to line your box with aluminum foil so you have an easy way to get the individual cubes out.

Incense is best used in combination with the anointing oils. Frankessence and Myrrh or Frankessence, Myrrh and Sandalwood make a lovely prosperity perfume or anointing oil. It has a deep, rich odor that is lush but not too sweet to be worn by a man, so *you* can use it regardless of your sex. A simple ritual that lights candles and Prosperity/Money Attracting Incense, then anoints your brow and heart with the rich smelling oil and follows up with the prosperity chant can set strong financial tides into motion for you.

How a Salesman Used the Ritual for Success

Here is a typical report from an elderly gentleman, C.R.: "I am a retail stationery and office supply salesman. I regularly call on relatively small business firms to supply their needs for standard forms, paper clips, transfer files and the like. This used to be a tough job that barely let me make ends meet. With a 'what have I got to lose' attitude, I tried the candles, incense, oil and Prosperity Chant one morning. That day, my customers seemed more friendly and cooperative than usual, and I got several referrals to potential new customers, including two people who called up other businesses and arranged appointments for me. It was a good enough day that I decided to give the little ritual another go the next morning. Again people seemed especially nice to me and I had a feeling of confidence and growing opulence—that Frankessence seems to turn me on anyway."

"So using the ritual, I had the best week, then the best month I've ever had in this business. My sales are continuing to pick up and I look forward both to my morning ritual and to the growing pleasure of associating with such nice business people. I seem to be constantly complimented on my pleasant personality and everybody seems to want to help my sales grow. Every night now, I have an extra ritual just to say thank you to the wonderful forces that are obviously helping me. I have all I want in a wardrobe, beautiful home and a new car, but best of all a richer, happier life. I don't tell many people about this. I guess it would sound like a bunch of silly superstition. But it works! And I'll tell you, I am happily hooked."

Prosperity Through Psychic Ecology

Let's pause for a metaphysical look at prosperity. Although we are working with more tangible techniques, all the basics of positive thinking still apply. If you get up from a wonderfully powerful prosperity ritual and fall back into the old habits of a poverty and lack complex, you'll surely blow the whole bit!

We are learning to build and activate powerful positive *thoughtforms,* but never forget that your habitual thinking produces strong *thoughtforms,* too. Since the world is finally coming around to an ecology binge, we should follow its example in our thought atmosphere. You may look around you at the polluted rivers, streams and air and know that man is making a mess out of his physical environment. But the unseen world is an even bigger mess—it is terribly polluted with thoughts of fear, lack, resentment, jealousy, anger and the other negative energies *that tend to block your good.* Pollutants in a river kill the fish, and in just the same way negative thought patterns will kill your most cherished dreams—often before you have completed your rituals!

YOUR PSYCHIC ECOLOGY BEGINS WITH YOU

What can YOU do about it? Even more than in the material world, *psychic ecology* must begin with the individual. And it's not enough just to stop polluting the thought atmosphere yourself. You must become a fountain of happiness and good cheer. Be quick with the warm smile and the ready wit. Carry happy tales of success and share a good joke as often as possible. Work to improve your opinion of yourself, of money, and of other people. Avoid negative people as diligently as you would avoid downtown on an exceptionally smoggy day.

The Mirror Ritual

But all that is simply common sense, we need a more positive program of personal psychic ecology. I like to call this the *mirror ritual.* At least once a week, try a session with yourself. Go to your altar and light the candles and incense. Anoint your brow and heart with oil. then take a good look in the mirror.

Address yourself to the image in the mirror as if it were you. Say something like: "Al (Use your own name, I used Al as if I were performing this ritual), you are a very wonderful and deserving person. You are obviously entitled to love, wealth, riches, happiness and great prosperity." Then be very quiet and listen to the answering thoughts. But never take, "That's ridiculous," or "Oh, no you are not," as an answer. If you get a negative reaction, deliberately provoke a dialog with the image. Say "Look here, a flip answer won't help us. If you don't agree with my statement, start giving me specific reasons why not." Then make notes, preferrably in writing, and *take action* to correct the valid ones.

Whether valid or not, harboring negative opinions of yourself is a blatant violation of all the rules of psychic ecology. For some of us, this mirror ritual can be a real cathartic exercise with psychological trauma from facing that which we have so carefully swept under the mental rug in the past. Treat the list of objections you get from your mirror in the same fashion that we worked on your carefully constructed guilt list in *Healing Yourself with ESP.* The principles are the same. Harboring the pollution of negative thoughts and opinions of yourself will hamper you forever unless you take positive actions to clean up the mess. But the clean-up is both fun and rewarding.

How a Young Man Used the Mirror Ritual for Success

At 22 Bill was a stock boy in a small department store. He appeared to be a sloppy bungler and was in danger of losing even the meager income from this beginning job. He tried the mirror ritual and got an astounding response. The image flashed him the critical thought, "You're no good. Remember when you were 16 and went out for football. You had to have that form notarized for school, so you went to the local stationery store and your father's friend notarized it, but you didn't pay him." Then Bill remembered—he hadn't known what a notary was much less that you were supposed to pay them. But he had been teased about it the next day and it went deep inside. So Bill wrapped a dollar bill in a note that simply said, "In payment of an old debt," and mailed it to the notary unsigned. After two more equally "trivial" objections from the mirror were corrected, Bill's work began to improve rapidly, so much so that he was soon promoted to the sales floor, and became a junior buyer within another year. As Bill would explain it, "It was my changed opinion of myself that made the whole difference."

Special Warnings in Using the Mirror Ritual

So when your mirror "speaks" to you, don't shrug off the "trivial" objections, they can be the key to nearly instant success! Put in its most positive light, the idea is to build up your sense of personal worth and worthiness. This is a solid part of strengthening the *faith* point of your witch's pyramid. Combined with your ever growing *constructive will, creative imagination* and the power of *secrecy,* your manifestation of happily increasing opulence is assured.

A Complete Money/Prosperity Attracting Ritual

Let's put it all together now in what could be the most important step of your life toward complete material and financial success. Planning and preparation are as important here as if you were applying for a million dollar grant from the government. And indeed the fully successful ritual could be worth more than that to you. The only limits are your feelings of worthiness and expectation of powerful results—and your ability to develop the right touch of the great power you are about to tap. Let's begin with a list of materials that should be made or purchased in advance:

1) Money Drawing Powder (see the recipe in Chapter 3)
2) Money Drawing Wash (see the recipe in this chapter)
3) Prosperity/Money Attracting Incense (see recipe in this chapter)
4) Prosperity Oil (Frankessence & Myrrh or Frankessence, Myrrh and Sandalwood)
5) A pair of green tapered candles for your candle holders.
6) Matches, a candle snuffer and the normal altar accessories.

Next plan your timing. This ritual should begin after the Moon has turned new and when it enters the astrological sign of Cancer, Scorpio or Pisces. (Astrological calendars or moon tables are available at any drug store or newsstand). Best results come when your ritual is repeated at the same time each night for eight consecutive days. If the Moon sign bit sounds too complicated, then just pay attention to when the next new moon occurs and plan to start your ritual work one evening later.

Physical preparation of your body and mind should be as careful as for the Love Attracting Ritual. The bath or shower with special attention to perfuming the body and beautifying the hair will impress the forces of prosperity quite as much as the forces of love. Now you are ready to come to your altar and begin the ritual itself.

Ritual Step #1: Smile at the face in your altar mirror and greet the room in general with a friendly Hi! Then build your protective white light—see or imagine a large sphere of white light with you safely at the center. Now turn the white light a lovely shade of rich green and chant:

> Rama, Agni, send the Light to me.
>> Rama, Agni, send the lush Green Light to me.
> Bathe me with your growth and love,
>> Send abundance from above.
> Rama, Agni, send the Light that sets me free.

As always, use each chant at least three times to get a feeling of real power from it.

Ritual Step #2: Light your candles and the Prosperity/Money-Attracting incense, then chant the Prosperity Chant:

> Oh, great and mighty Jupiter, your friendship I do seek.
>> Your emissaries send to me, spirits rich and sleek.
> Good nature spirits sent by Jove, your comradeship I love.
>> For bounty and good fellowship, my thanks are sent above.
> Spirits great, your riches share in fun and friendship true,
>> Prosperity descends on me, my thanks to lovely you.
> And now my Light is shining bright, rich green for all to see.
>> Good fortune is my law of life. With thanks, so mote it be!

Ritual Step #3: Anoint your brow and heart with Prosperity oil and lightly sprinkle money drawing powder on your altar and the surrounding area as you chant:

> My words, have power as of old,

So hear me now, good Gnomes and Trolls.
Bring me silver, bring me gold,
      Bring the lush green stuff that folds.
Come quickly now, have fun with me,
      And treasure bring most happily.
I speak to you with joy and glee,
      And as my will, so mote it be!

Ritual Step #4: Lightly sprinkle your altar and surrounding area with the Money Drawing Wash as you use this modification of the chant:

Nature spirits hark to me,
      Bring me opportunity
Bring me windfalls as good fun,
      Winning horses one by one.
Rising stocks, good poker hands,
      Gifts of diamonds, platinum bands
Bring it gladly now to me,
      And as my will, so mote it be.

Ritual Step #5: This is the time to build a really powerful *thoughtform*. Hold out your hands and start the energy flowing between them. Mentally mould it into a tall, wide funnel shaped channel. Now see the channel filling with money for you. As you keep the energy flowing, visualize aloud:

The channel for my prosperity is built and is now being filled with
Rainbows and waves, rivers and streams, buckets and wheelbarrows full
      of money.
It rains down on me in an ever increasing flow of riches and abundance.
And I give my thanks to all the *thoughtforms* and spirits who are
      helping.

Spend as much time as you need to enjoy the full living reality of your *thoughtform*, then touch it lovingly and release it to its life of effectiveness for you.

Ritual Step #6: Invite your nature spirit friends to come along. Put on enough clothing to go outside. Walk three times around your house or apartment (if this is impossible, go around as much of the place as you can) while lightly sprinkling the Money Drawing Wash and repeating the chant. Follow this with another three trips around the house as you lightly sprinkle the Money Drawing Powder and use its chant.

Ritual Step #7: Return to your altar and feed your *thought-form* with love as you once more "visualize aloud" the rivers and streams, buckets and wheelbarrows of money.

Ritual Step #8: Close the ritual. Use the snuffer to turn off your candles, then thank and dismiss the spirits and elementals, "My thanks to all spirits and elementals who have participated here. Go now to perform your appointed tasks, and when you are finished, return to your natural homes, harming no one on the way. Peace, love and thanks to all. Blessed be."

PRACTICAL BENEFITS FROM THIS RITUAL

The results from this ritual are often what people call the once in a lifetime opportunity—but the "biggies" *keep happening* to those who generate the deep feeling and power that is possible here.

How J.Y. Closed a Million Dollar Deal

J.Y. was 68. Three years ago he had gone through a painful and expensive divorce that left him with a feeling of no reason to live. He turned to drink and woke up one morning after several months on "skid row" with the decision that it was time to face life again. He cleaned himself up and contacted friends with the hope of getting some management consulting work. There were a few odd jobs, but too many people felt he was "all washed up" and "over the hill."

One thing he had plenty of was time, so he decided to try the full prosperity ritual I taught him. On the morning of the fourth day, a friend called to suggest that a local business was for sale and needed a bit of promotion. An appointment was arranged and J. received a $2,000 retainer and a contract for a 3 percent commission upon sale of the business. For less than 20 hours work and $150 postage, a buyer was found at a price close to a million dollars. The nearly $30,000 commission financed a swank new office and launched a whole new career for J. I can testify to this personally because the gentleman brought the commission check to my office to show me.

How B.J. Put His Ailing Corporation over the Top

It had been almost five years in an exotic part of the electronics business, and the little company was still in serious trouble. It was badly undercapitalized at the start, and subsequent losses had produced a negative net worth of about $50,000. Most men would have given up and let the creditors pick over the bones of the dead business. But the founder, B.J., wasn't ready to quit. He used the Complete Money/Prosperity Attracting Ritual with the idea of obtaining fresh capital for the business. His intent was to continue the repetition of the ritual every night until something happened.

On the morning of the 4th day, B.J. received a phone call suggesting that a local S.B.I.C. (Small Business Investment Company) might be interested in making a loan. He followed up immediately, and secured a $20,000 loan to tide the company over the negotiations. Within 6 weeks, he had successfully concluded a loan of $250,000—Still showing a negative net worth! Within another two years, he sold the company to a New York Stock Exchange listed firm for something over a million dollars.

CHAPTER POINTS TO REMEMBER

1) The greatest power of witchcraft comes from the running love affair with the spirit forces of nature. Woo the nature spirits, and good fortune and wealth will be showered upon you constantly.

2) The money drawing wash is wonderful for increasing business or attracting good tenants for your apartments. Use it and enjoy financial growth.

3) Money drawing powder used with the chant attracts the lucky breaks in business or job changing, good hunches on the horses, and all manner of financial good fortune. Use it regularly.

4) Make or at least use the prosperity incense and oils. This is especially useful in sales and promotional work, but it has many "lucky" side effects.

5) Practice the mirror ritual and clean up your psychic atmosphere—it brings much success on its own and should be considered a prerequisite to using the complete prosperity ritual.

6) The Complete Money/Prosperity Attracting Ritual is a financial blockbuster. Use it with joy and expectation and become covered with wealth!

Chapter Eight

Incantations, Rituals and
Spells as Used in
Health Matters

Now that you have the power to attract fulfilling love and boundless riches, let's turn our attention to maintaining a healthy body in which to enjoy them. There is another good reason to seek vibrant health—the more vital your body, the stronger will be your spell casting ability; or shall we say, the more powerful will be your ritual work.

AN EFFECTIVE WITCH IS CAREFUL OF DIET

To produce an extra measure of the magnetic energy that powers *thoughtforms* and spells you must give your body enough good care to exhibit greater than average resilience and vitality. Please don't expect me to give you some sort of special fad diet in the name of Witchcraft. Quite the contrary, we are individuals and our individual bodies require special amounts of very different foods. Some Witches are vegetarians, others are heavy meat eaters—vibrant health comes from gaining a rapport with your body that is sufficient to understand and supply its needs including food, rest, recreation and thought.

Have you ever caught a lovely lady in the grocery store surreptitiously checking out a melon with a pendulum? She wasn't necessarily a Witch, but the pendulum or a similar technique for checking on the quality or digestibility of a food (for *you*) is a perfectly natural Witch tool. Nutty as my friends tease me that I am, I don't carry a pendulum to the local grocery store, but I find it useful to ask a melon or pineapple if it is ripe and would like to be a useful part of my diet. The answer comes from holding the palm of my left hand over the questioned item—there is a definite flow of energy to a yes answer, and it ignores you completely if it is not for you. And what energy do I feel? It's the same stuff that we build our *thoughtforms* out of! So *you* already have the power to communicate with fruits and vegetables. Try it! Since I have been talking to them, I've never wasted good money on a bad papaya, cantaloupes, mango, pineapple or honeydew melon, and neither will you! And you can extend this concept in the right manner to asking any food or prepared dish if it will agree with you. Result! No more indigestion.

Let's close our discussion of physical diet by repeating the suggestion that you get to know your body and its needs much better. The secret of good diet is in letting your body tell you what it needs and can handle well—never take somebody else's "canned" diet as something right for you. Instead ask, and learn about your body's needs from the best informed of all sources, the foods and your body itself.

YOUR THOUGHT DIET AND BREATH SYSTEM

But food and drink are only a small segment of your daily intake. Pay careful heed to the thoughts your mind feeds upon also. In our last chapter, we spent a good deal of time on Psychic Ecology, and you will find its principles of infinite value to your physical as well as financial health. So, does that finish our discussion of the body's intake? The science of *breath* requires equal consideration with its companion sciences of diet and thought! Whether or not you like the Vedantic concept of *Prana*, you must understand that breath is the most necessary requirement to sustain human life. We can go for weeks without food and days without water, but only for minutes without breath!

THE MYSTERIOUS POWER OF BREATH FOR YOUR LUNGS

The average American breathes with the top part of the chest through the front of the nose, thereby using less than half of the available lung capacity.

Typical of this is a lady, D.R., who asked for help with an asthmatic condition. The various medications the Doctors had given her were loaded with side effects that to her seemed worse than the original condition. It took s˙ fifteen minute sessions over a two-week period to teach her to breathe through the back of her nose into the lower diaphram. (After all, she was 60 and her breathing habits were pretty solidly set.) With the use of the extra lung capicity and a bit of healing Light, she eliminated her chronic cough as well as all the medicines. Result: she has more energy, looks younger and dances through life without the worries and side effects of strong medicines—full breathing brought a healing that all manner of medications couldn't touch.

How about you? Are you using your nature given lung capacity to the fullest? Try this simple test: put your hand flat against your waist, with half above and half below the belt line on your *back.* Now take a deep breath. If you don't feel the lower back muscles moving straight back as you inhale, you are missing the most important part of your lung area! Practice making the air produce a funny sound in the back of your nose as your back muscles pull the life giving air deep into your body—the fresh invigoration of success is its own reward here. Just as an aside: often a newcomer to our classes at E.S.P. Lab will comment on the funny noise when I take a deep breath before chanting—the classic remark was, "It sounded like somebody was blowing up a balloon." You will know when you are breathing properly by the noise it makes, and the extra vitality it gives you.

WATER AND HERBS FOR YOUR HEALTH

In the great Witchcraft traditions pure water can be changed by the spirit forces to bring the trace chemicals needed by your body for vibrant health. The good Witch or occultist will put a fresh glass of water on the nightstand at bed time. Traditionally you hold your hands palm down over the water to help direct vital energy into it as you chant:

THE WATER CHANT FOR HEALTH

Oh, spirits mine, this water pure is put here for your use.
    To bring my body chemicals for health placed in this juice.
My loving thanks I send to you for help you give to me.
    My vibrant health is certain now, thanks, and so mote it be!

Next morning just as you arise, repeat the chant while again directing the energy into the water with your hands. Then drink it all right down regardless of how it tastes. Some people get strange flavors in the morning, but that should be taken as a sure sign that your spirit friends are helping.

A Case History

B.C. sent us an ecstatic report on this simple ritual: "I have been overweight for longer than I care to remember, but the water ritual has brought me the help and incentive to get my girlish figure back. The first morning as I completed the ritual started the night before, I'd swear that water tasted like pure iodine! But I got the feeling of help with my weight. I continued the ritual each evening and morning, and the water still tasted awful, but by the end of the first week I had lost five pounds! And I lost five pounds a week for five full weeks. Now I am just the dress size I want to be, and the water has quit tasting so terrible in the mornings. But you can be sure I will continue this ritual for life—I love my new figure."

HERBAL WITCHCRAFT PRACTICE

Do you have another glass? Let's add a touch of pure herbal witchcraft to run in parallel with the water ritual. Try an ounce of horehound, an ounce of ash leaves, an ounce of peppermint leaves and a tablespoon of salt. Crush and mix it all well in your mortar and pestle while chanting:

> Spirits of life and health, I ask
> Renew my body for its tasks.
> Make me strong and full of glee.
> My hearty thanks I give to thee.

Each evening at bedtime, put half a teaspoon of your herb mixture into the extra glass of water, hold your hands over it and repeat the health chant three times. In the morning, throw the mixture away because it has already done its work. During the night the herbs give off essences that both attract health giving nature spirits and have a healing effect of their own.

A CASE OF RELIEF RECEIVED FROM THE RITUAL

Used in connection with the deep diaphragmatic breathing, this simple ritual can work wonders. Here is a typical report from

C.R.: "As you know, my doctor called it Emphysema and I experienced great weakness from the inability to absorb oxygen with my lungs. I have been using the water ritual and the health herb ritual along with three ten minute periods of deep diaphragmatic breathing each day. There has been a steady improvement in my condition that I sense every day. It has been six weeks now and the difference is virtually unbelievable. I can even run or climb stairs without falling limp into the nearest chair for an hour like before. The rituals seem too simple to do much good, but *they work* for me"!

SEASONING AND HERB TEAS FOR HEALTH

Just as the superstition about a black cat being bad luck comes from age-old common knowledge of the negative aspects of Witchcraft, so the healing power of herbs in teas and seasoning comes to us from times past when medicine itself was a form of the occult arts. As a Witch or metaphysician, I have no quarrel with the modern medical profession. If I'm ever dumb enough to break a leg, I'll certainly have a doctor set it first—then I'll try to amaze him at the speed of the recovery. Let's stress again that a good Witch is definitely an eclectic and there is no reason to avoid a doctor if you know you're sick. But preventative herbal rituals can save much misery and medical expense.

The ancient Chinese practice of the Acupuncture Doctor fits nicely into the idea we are trying to impart here. Traditionally, the patient paid the Acupuncture Doctor a regular retainer for preventative treatment and health advice. But if he got sick, the Doctor paid him!

Most health food stores carry commercially packaged herb teas reputed to calm the nerves, eliminate excess body fluids, purify the blood, aid digestion and all sorts of good things. Before you dismiss this as hogwash, remember some of Grandma's home remedies that worked when you were a tiny tot! Peppermint tea is definitely a natural aid to digestion—you find this updated in modern medicine as the after meals mint pill so often prescribed for an ulcer patient. Sassafras, sarsaparilla and horehound have health giving properties in teas also and it will pay you to experiment with all of them. At least you'll find it healthy to substitute some of the natural teas for part of the coffee that most of us consume in great excess. It is amazing how some of the 19th century "old wives' remedies" have real merit if you give them a chance. And there's no danger of penicillin reaction or the like from the natural herbs.

Many of our traditional food seasonings also came to us from the herbal lore of witchcraft. Here's a place where we can all enjoy good Witchcraft—tastier food as an aid to health! Thyme, hops, peppermint, sassafras, bay laurel and basil have found their way into the gourmet cookbooks. All these have a Witchcraft aura of healing along with the happy fallout of enhancing the flavor of your food. And of course the classic Italian Witch uses oregano in almost everything. I must have had an Italian Witch incarnation because I instinctively use oregano not just in salads but to liven up my meats and vegetables as well.

HERBS IN OUR DRINKING HABITS

The helpful herbs have found their way even into our drinking habits. Angustora Bitters are a must for any well stocked bar, for instance. But it's amazing how well they settle your stomach. When I was barely 21 I went to my Uncle's wedding up in Santa Barbara. The champagne flowed a bit too freely for my tender years, and as I sort of flowed toward the door for the drive back to Los Angeles, the old bartender collared me and said: "Wait a minute! You're not going anywhere in that condition." He dragged me back to the bar and made a concoction of bitters, a dash of lime juice and soda water. He shoved it at me with a, "Here! Drink this." It didn't taste bad at all and it really straightened me out.

BENEFITS OF WITCHCRAFT HERBS

Let's close this section with the challenge to be a good eclectic. Experiment with the teas and seasonings not just for flavor, but to add the zest of vibrant health to your daily life. J.S. was the tensed up nervous stomach type business man who had flirted with an ulcer for years. His friends described him as a twenty cup of coffee and three packs of cigarettes a day man. Jumpy was an understatement, he reminded you of the character so beautifully portrayed by Don Knotts! When a routine physical caused the doctor to threaten him with an ulcer diet or worse, J.S. decided to experiment with the herb teas. He hit upon a mixture of sassafras and peppermint that tasted pretty good so he used it at home—2 cups at breakfast and 2 cups after dinner. Here is his enthusiastic report: "I feel great! With the help of the herb tea, I'm down to four cups of coffee and less than a pack of cigarettes a day. But the good part is that I'm not nervous anymore. Things that used to blow my stack just get handled. It's amazing how comfortable life can be when you're relaxed enough to enjoy it"!

How to Make Sachets for Feeling Better

We're back to the turn of the century again. You are probably too young to have experienced it, but I'll bet you can remember Grandma griping about the asafetida bag her mother made her wear to school. The garlic necklace and/or asafetida bag to ward off colds and other contagious diseases was a trademark of the early 1900's in rural America—and it worked! Grandma survived to raise your parents—or was it in spite of the awful odors? In the "old days," a Bull Durham bag made an ideal sachet bag, but since most modern smokers use "tailor made" cigarettes, you will probably have to make yours out of scrap cloth. A flat bag one inch by 1 1/2 inches is about right, and even a helpless male can sew well enough to make one.

I'm not going to suggest that you fill it with something as odiferous as garlic or asafetida; but eucalyptus, vervain and mandrake root make a good sachet that won't embarrass you in public. I'll confess that I don't normally carry a health sachet myself, but if you were to shake me down you would find four different protective stones, and pieces of mandrake root and John the Conqueror in my pockets along with a protective ankh on a chain around my neck—but most of that comes in a later chapter. And don't go by my example alone—I'm the "disgustingly healthy" variety anyway. If you are not, then you can use all the extra help you can get.

Building a Health Consciousness Thoughtform

Let's clear the way for the complete health ritual by working on your health consciousness. Here we turn back to basic metaphysics for a strong foundation. I'll always remember an old gentleman whose approach to life was: "The fellow said, 'Cheer up, things could be worse.' So I cheered up, and sure enough, they did get worse." I never wondered why he was sick all the time—he did it to himself with his negative thinking. In my book, *Helping Yourself with ESP,* the health chapter includes a Table of Mental Poisons and their Symptoms. If your knowledge of basic metaphysics or positive thinking is the least bit weak, you will be well served by reviewing that whole health chapter. For the here and now, let's just remind you that harboring negative thought/reaction patterns is much like drinking sulphuric acid—you might get away with small quantities for a while, but it's deadly at best.

Most of us are too busy trying to win the Irish Sweepstakes, beat the ponies or launch a fresh love affair, to spend the time necessary to take good care of our health. But what good is five million dollars in the bank and the world's best lover mad about you if you're too sick to enjoy it? The best time to work on your health consciousness is not when your body is full of pain, but when you feel *good!* We must stress that your *thoughtform* will gather energy and substance according to the quality of the energy that you pump into it. Take care to feed it on vibrant health. The alternative is to amplify the very pain you seek to eliminate. Here the student asks: "But how can I get well if I can't build the health *thoughtform* while I'm sick"? Unless you have a chronic illness it is indeed better to postpone your work until you are feeling "in the pink." Regardless of your present physical condition, the technique is the same, but the more health you have to put in, the better will be the power for attracting health in your *thoughtform.*

So let's talk about technique. Start by building or imagining the protective sphere of white Light in which you sit safely. Now turn it to the color blue that corresponds to the blue of an electric spark. Hold out your hands and build the *thoughtform* energy between them, coloring it electric blue as you go. Begin to program it with the Health *Thoughtform* Chant:

AN EFFECTIVE HEALTH THOUGHTFORM CHANT

Goddesses
Gods of beauty and of Light,
  Hear my call this lovely night.
Your gift of health I seek to share,
  Hold me in your loving care.
This *thoughtform* that we build in blue,
  Nurtures me and keeps me, too,

> Safe from accident or harm,
>   Living out a life of charm.
> Vibrant health shall be my lot,
>   Sickness is what I have not.
> Fresh cloak of blue this *thoughtform* be,
>   Ever more protecting me.
> With vital life my body fills,
>   Leaving room for no more ills.
> Perfect health for all to see,
>   And as my will, so mote it be!

As the chant continues, let the *thoughtform* grow until it spontaneously reaches out to begin its work—feel it surround, protect and vitalize your body. And wear it everywhere in perfect health. I suggested to one of our students that she think of her *thoughtform* cloak as a suit of shining blue armor, and she took me literally. A few weeks later, she appeared in class obviously enjoying great health and vitality. Her opening remark was, "I sure enjoy that suit of blue armor plate. It's amazing the way it works. Many times during the day, I hear a little clinking noise as the germs and thought barbs that used to make me sick hit my armor plate and bounce harmlessly off. I'm exposed to the same people, colds, tensions and hostility as before, but now it all just clinks against my armor and falls harmlessly off. I'm a new woman!"

The living reality that she built is the key. If your *thoughtform* armor is solid enough that you hear those clinks, I can guarantee your success—but if you are more of a figurative thinker, then trust your *thoughtform* to work without clinking and you can still enjoy its perfect protection. The trick is to avoid poking holes in your armor from the inside where it is soft. Anger, resentment, cynicism or jealousy inside will blow your *thoughtform* to bits. Protect it from these and it will happily reciprocate by protecting you from all external harm.

COMPLETE HEALTH PROTECTION AND RESTORATION RITUAL

Let's begin by listing the items needed in addition to your regular goodies:

1) Health attracting oil (rose, carnation, citron, gardenia or any combination).

2) Health attracting incense (Use the recipe as for money/

attracting incense in Chapter 7, but substitute one or two of the floral scents for the Frankessence and Myrrh).

3) A chalice or cup of water with the horehound, ash, peppermint, salt mixture (about 1/2 teaspoon of the herb mixture in a cup of water).

4) Two blue tapered candles for your altar candle holders.

5) Your regular nightstand glass full of pure water.

Your love affair with life and the nature spirits carries over naturally into this ritual. Prepare for your date with the health forces of nature with the same care you would prepare to meet your favorite sex symbol human being. Take the precautions to be sure you are not interrupted and go to your altar.

Now the ritual itself:

Ritual Step #1: Smile at the face in your altar mirror and happily greet your spirit friends in the room. Begin by setting your protection of Light. Picture that powerful sphere of white Light all around you, then turn it electric blue and chant:

> Rama, Agni, send the Light to me.
> Rama, Agni, send Electric Blue to me.
> Heal my body and affairs.
> Bring creative thought to bear.
> Rama, Agni, send the Light that sets me free.

(As always, use each chant three or more times—until it feels right to you.)

Ritual Step #2: Light your candles and incense. Then hold your hands palms down over the glass of water to send energy into it, and chant:

> Oh spirits mine, this water pure is put here for your use.
> To bring my body chemicals for health placed in this juice.
> My loving thanks I send to you for help you give to me.
> My vibrant health is certain now, thanks, and so mote it be!

Ritual Step #3: Anoint your brow, throat and heart with the health oil and chant:

> And now this oily essence fair
> Adds its great power to the air
> Attracting spirits of the Light,

> Bringing health both day and night.
> This charge is true and proper, see,
> And as my will, so mote it be!

Ritual Step #4: Sprinkle your health herb/water lightly on your altar and the surrounding area as you chant:

> Spirits of life and health, I ask,
> Renew my body for its tasks.
> Make me strong and full of glee.
> My hearty thanks I give to thee.

Ritual Step #5: Hold out your hands and start to build the *thoughtform* between them. Watch it, and feel it grow up to become your suit of life giving blue armor plate as you chant:

> Gods of beauty and of Light,
> Hear my call this lovely night.
> Your gift of health I seek to share,
> Hold me in your loving care.
> This *thoughtform* that we build in blue
> Nurtures me and keeps me, too,
> Safe from accident or harm,
> Living out a life of charm.
> Vibrant health shall be my lot,
> Sickness is what I have not.
> Fresh cloak of blue this *thoughtform* be,
> Ever more protecting me.
> With vital life my body fills,
> Leaving room for no more ills.
> Perfect health for all to see,
> And as my will, so mote it be!

When you feel the complete life and power built in your *thoughtform* you are ready to to on to the next step. Spend as much time as it takes here to *know* that the *thoughtform* has reached a full and vibrant life of its own.

Ritual Step #6: Again hold your hands palms down over the glass of water and feel the energy flowing into it as you use the chant:

> Oh spirits mine, this water pure is put here for your use

To bring my body chemicals for health placed in this juice.
My loving thanks I send to you for help you give to me.
My vibrant health is certain now, thanks, so mote it be!

When it feels ready, toast your spirit friends with the glass and drink it down.

Ritual Step #7: Close your ritual with thanks as usual: "My loving thanks to all spirits and elementals who have participated here. To the elementals, I dismiss you in love to perform your appointed tasks. When you are finished, return in peace in your native habitats and harm no one on the way. Again my loving thanks to all for your help and love. Blessed be." Then use your candle snuffer to extinguish the candles and the ritual is complete.

Here is a simple case reported in good faith to us. Bonnie went to the doctor and was told that she had a fibroid tumor "in a very personal and inconvenient place." A second examination was scheduled for a week later to set a date for the operation. But Bonnie had some ideas of her own about this. Of course she asked for prayers from all the people and organizations she could think of, but she topped it off with this complete health protection and restoration ritual. For seven straight nights, she worked. Then on the morning of the eighth day she returned to the doctor—there was no trace of the tumor!

Maybe it's because I have a soft spot in my heart for the tradition of the ancient Chinese Acupuncture Doctors, but my favorite type of feedback from this part of the work is not a healing. Rather it is the year after year report that says, "I continue in vibrantly perfect health." Keep up the love affair with life and health, and use the health ritual at least on each new moon—and make health a constant fact for YOU. Witchcraft can demonstrate this very effectively for you.

CHAPTER POINTS TO REMEMBER

1) Vibrant health is necessary to generate the greatest power for your rituals and spells.

2) We are all different in our body requirements and tolerances. Don't get carried away by somebody else's fad diet. Study yourself and learn what foods are best. You can often ask a melon if it is ripe and will agree with your system—ask and hold out your

left hand, palm down over the item. A yes answer will produce a definite energy flow, just like the *thoughtform* energy that you have learned to build between your hands.

3) There is more to diet than merely food. Take care of your thought intake as well as your breathing. Deep diaphragmatic breathing brings in extra quantities of life giving energy that repairs and vitalizes your body.

4) The nightly water ritual, reenforced by nightly use of the health herbs in the second glass of water will go a long way toward insuring your health.

5) Experiment with the herb teas and seasonings. You can stay healthy and have better tasting food at the same time.

6) A ritually prepared sachet can be useful in protecting you when you have to go around people who may have colds or other communicable diseases.

7) The health consciousness *thoughtform* will work literally as a suit of armor if you build it that way. But it is quite effective in the less solid form—as long as you feel its living reality around you.

8) Use the complete ritual to protect your health at least once a month—the night of the new moon is best—and live a healthy, happy life until it comes your turn to be released comfortably to the higher planes of life.

Chapter Nine

How to Ward Off the Evil Eye and Protect Yourself Against Secret Psychic Attack

*H*ad a run of bad luck lately? Any strange aches and pains that the doctor can't explain? Do you often feel shut out, depressed or unwanted? Are you listless, depleted or feeling unusual compulsions? Of course there may be a "logical" explanation, but all of these may be symptoms of psychic attack. The evil eye and psychic attack may seem ridiculous, in this second half of the Twentieth Century, but they are *real* and more prevalent than you think. To ignore psychic self-defense is to leave yourself open to disaster and unhappiness that need not be your lot.

HOW A WIDOW OVERCAME PSYCHIC ATTACK

An attractive widow, E.R., had made a few visits to an occult group. When she realized that they were dabbling in black magic, she quit. And suddenly her world seemed to blow up in her face—unexpected debts suddenly materialized against her husband's estate, the Internal Revenue Service made a big assessment based on audit of her husband's tax returns, she had a series of minor accidents around the house, and even her 13-year-old son who had been a model boy suddenly became cantankerous and totally uncooperative. Within three months she was reduced to a state of utter despair. After a soul-searching discussion with me she tried the complete ritual we will give at the close of this chapter. It took nine full days to be sure that the negative influence over her was broken. Life slowly returned to normal and she began to work herself out of her "unexplained bad luck." Then her love ritual work performed later attracted a new husband, and we could say "they lived happily ever after" all due to her using the powers of White Witchcraft.

Let's begin a groundwork of understanding to insure your future freedom from the miseries and disaster of psychic attack.

UNDERSTANDING THE MANY DEGREES
AND SHADINGS OF PSYCHIC ATTACK

Any exercise of control by one person over another can logically be classified as psychic attack. There are many levels of control and attack, beginning with very simple things—for instance the elevator bit that was demonstrated on the TV show, Candid Camera. It was a harmless joke, but it clearly demonstrates the power of control by group action. They let the "victim" enter the elevator, then three staff members followed him. The staff members faced the back wall, and very quickly the "victim" turned to face the wall too. Then when they all turned around, he quickly followed suit. When the staff members took off their hats, he took off his hat. And when they all put their hats back on, again the "victim" conformed. There is a tremendous power to group pressure that controls an individual. How many times have you bought a "far out" bit of clothing and then let it stay in the closet because you were "afraid" to wear it? Why?

Part of the answer appeared in I.B.M.'s interesting magazine, *THINK*, in late 1969. The lead line to the article read something like: An Invisible Force Pushed the Professor to the Wall and Held Him There. The professor involved made a perfect "victim" since he is a Ph.D. in Psychology and so "should have known better." As the story unfolds, we find that the class worked up this experiment in group control without disclosing the plan to the professor. When class began, the students gave the professor their rapt attention as long as he moved to his left, but every time he started to his right they would rustle papers, drop pencils and murmur to each other. The subsconscious effect of this reward and punishment propelled the professor to the corner of the room at his left in less than ten minutes, and he gave the entire balance of his lecture from the corner. This classic technique is used on you all the time. Wives have been training husbands this way for centuries!

Take a good look at the simple ways that people use to manipulate you. A warm response when you do something they like, or as one gentleman put it, "My ex-wife had an uncanny ability to drop the temperature in the room by twenty degrees when I did something she didn't like"! Psychology has already recognized the simple techniques of control, but it has much to learn about the stronger methods—projection of moods, aggressive attack by well-built *thoughtforms,* blatantly erotic *thoughtforms,* and obsession by powerful negative spirit entities. If a cloud of "bad luck" seems to follow you, it's time to quit blaming "bad karma" and learn some positive psychic defense.

HOW TO RECOGNIZE PSYCHIC ATTACK
OR ATTEMPTS TO CONTROL YOU BY PSYCHIC MEANS

We must begin with the basics. Whether it be three persons jokingly causing you to turn around in an elevator or a powerfully constructed slashing psychic attack, the techniques of recognition are the same. And recognition is still the key. If you don't recognize it, you become its puppet. And you will dance on the strings until you recognize the need for counter measures. Let's establish three simple rules for recognition of attack or control directed at you:

Rule #1: **Challenge All Suggestions!** There are many shadings of negative suggestion directed to you during the course of a day or week. Most of us have learned to resist the advertising type thing that implies failure if you don't use "Lardy Hair Preparation" at least twice a day. And besides, those come from radio or TV where we have learned to keep our guard up to resist the flamboyant commercial message. But what of the competitor who eyes you confidently and says, "You might as well give up, 'cause I'm going to beat you anyway."? Or the friendly, "You're too old for that, Charlie." Or the, "Gee you don't look so good this morning" gambit?

Even positive suggestions can be designed to deliberately control you. For example, "I just gave $5 to the office collection for Susie, how about you"? The point to this discussion is to make you aware of your normal degree of vulnerability to the suggestion of others. The more easily you are influenced, the more important it becomes to have a set of powerful psychic defenses.

Let's add a footnote to this first rule. Some books will tell you that part of the power of a spell or psychic attack is generated by letting you know that you are to be attacked. *Don't* swallow that one either! Only the very suggestible can be caused to hurt themselves by the extra anxiety and bumbling they generate by accepting the outward suggestion. *Secrecy* is still one of the basic points of the Witch's pyramid of manifestation, and it is the *secret spell* that is most dangerous and harmful.

Rule #2: **Examine All Urges and Negative Feelings.** When a person slips you even a subtle suggestion, there is at least some natural knowledge of the suggestion's source. But "in person" suggestion is child's play and lacks the effectiveness of the projected mood, fear, or urge. It is altogether possible for a person to sit quietly at home and fill your psychic atmosphere with hatred and bitterness, either unconsciously or by negative ritual work. We will cover the positive aspects of such ritual work in Chapter 11, but you need the sensitivity and ability to defend yourself first.

To be safe, you need a habit of mentally inventorying your moods and their tendencies regularly. The sooner you spot a control *thoughtform* sent by somebody else, the less damage it can do before you kill it. I used to call this technique *a mental radar sweep of your aura*, and that is a sound method, but there is a more effective way: use your creative imagination to project your consciousness to the ceiling for a moment. And from that totally objective vantage point, look down at the being in your body and study the forces that are at work on it. AS long as you accept all of your feelings as your own, you will remain a puppet for those of strong will who control you by projecting what *they* want you to do next as your own desire.

John O. suddenly realized that his marriage was near the breaking point. He began to seek understanding by projecting himself to the ceiling to see what caused the now constant bickering with his wife, Martha. He quickly realized thereby that *he was the aggressor,* and Martha was merely defending herself. A little more analysis showed that the picky *thoughtforms* were coming from a young girl at his office who had obviously set her cap for him just about the time the trouble started. John didn't bother to mention the source, but he apologized to Martha for his picky attitude of the last two months and asked her help in recognizing it before it got out of hand. Less than two weeks of practice built an immunity to these control *thoughtforms,* and John and Martha entered a new stage of marital bliss much like a second honeymoon. Constant vigilance is the price of a life uncontrolled by the projected ulterior desires of others.

Rule #3: **Study All Fleeting Pains or Aches.** Common to the Huna, Voodo, and Black Witchcraft is a form of vengeful attack most often called "blocking your paths." This is accomplished by a powerful *thoughtform* (or even a group of lower entities) that operates in much the same way as pouring dirt into the gas tank of your car. It muddies your psychic energy centers and makes your aura so uncomfortable that even your closest friends tend to turn on you. As this spell or *thoughtform* attaches itself to you, it produces a series of fleeting aches and pains—little pains that quite obviously have no physical origin and so tend to be shrugged off as "nothing."

Another strong indication of such an attack is a "run of bad luck." When a bunch of little things all seem to go wrong at the same time, take action just as if you had noted the fleeting pains. Swiftness in reacting by conducting a full protection ritual will avoid much unnecessary misery. Never let the negative influences get a whole day's start on you. React quickly!

How Harry S. Protected Himself

A young salesman, Harry S. casually noted a few fleeting pains in his head, neck and stomach at breakfast, but he ignored them. When leaving the apartment for his first morning call, he found the driveway partially blocked by a poorly parked car, but he maneuvered around it OK and set out. There were several near misses in traffic, but he arrived at his first appointment safely— only to find a parking ticket on his car after an unsuccessful presentation. This was enough to convince Harry that he was in trouble. He hurried home and spent a half hour performing the complete protection ritual (as we give it in this chapter). There was a feeling of fresh confidence as he left the apartment this time with no obstructions, and he went on to close more sales that afternoon than he had all the previous week. Several days later, he was able to verify that an ex-girl friend had performed a negative ritual on him the evening before his miserable morning. But even without the verification, Harry was happy with the results of his protection ritual. You can do the same regarding your problems.

How Voodoo Attack Was Handled

A professional medium gave this account of an attack on her: "A lady brought me a voodoo doll as a gift and set it on the ledge over my fireplace. At first I thought it was sort of cute. Suddenly everything left me—my energy, my psychic ability and everything—I entered a very fretful state and in less than two hours I had a high fever and was bedridden. Then I lost all consciousness. When I woke, I looked up at that doll and realized that it was causing my misery. I crawled out of bed, grabbed the broom handle and knocked it down. Then I put it in a paper sack and set it outside, and did my White Witchcraft protective ritual. Almost immediately my strength returned, my fever left, and I went to the kitchen and cooked myself a big meal. When the woman who gave the doll to me came back, she wanted to bring it back into the house. I refused and told her it was evil and should be destroyed. She took it with her, but before she got home she was in a traffic accident."

If you stay alert with White Witchcraft, attacks even from voodoo sources can't conquer you.

A Ritual for Protection of Your Home

Materials for the home protection ritual should be assembled in advance: (1) A sachet bag—that you make or buy (2) A clove of garlic (3) A large piece of John the Conqueror—or powdered if you prefer, one heaping tablespoon will do (4) Mandrake root—a large piece or a teaspoon of the powder (5) Basil leaves or powder—a teaspoon full (6) Bay Laurel leaves or powder—a teaspoon full (7) Your normal altar supply of candles, protection incense, protection oil, matches, etc.

The ritual should be performed at midnight on the night of the full moon. Begin with the first four steps of the Basic Protection Ritual (see Chapter 2). In place of Step 5, begin to fill your sachet bag with the John the Conqueror, Garlic, Mandrake root, Basil, and Bay Leaves as you chant:

HOME PROTECTION RITUAL CHANT

Vishnu, Odin, Amon Ra,
   Shiva, Agni, Mighty Thor,
Spirits great and of goodwill,
   I know that you will fill the bill.
Defend this house against all harm,
   Protect it with your wit and charm.
In faith and trust I call to thee,
   And as my will, so mote it be!

When the sachet is full, put on enough clothing to go outside. Take the sachet in your two hands held in front of you, and march slowly three times around the outside of the house as you continually repeat the Home Protection Ritual Chant. When the three circuits of the house are completed, bring the sachet inside and hang it above the front door, while still chanting. Then return to your altar and close the ritual with dismissal of the elementals and thanks to all as usual.

How an Apartment Was Protected from Prowlers

H.L. lives in what she describes as a "tough neighborhood," and for obvious reasons we won't mention the name of the city. Here is her report after a year: "I use the Home Protection Ritual on every full moon as you suggested. This is my report after a full year. I live in an eight-unit apartment house and during the year, each of the other apartments has been broken into and robbed at least once, and one of them three times. My apartment is as vulnerable as the others but it has been left completely alone, so I thank all the spirits and the Ritual Deities every day for my wonderful protection. I'll use the protective ritual every full moon because I know what it has done for me."

The Power of Passive Defense

The Home Protection Ritual helps to keep you in a safe atmosphere, but we have seen that attack comes in many forms, so more defensive tools are needed. Witchcraft is a field where the well-known saying of General Robert E. Lee, "The best defense is attack," certainly does *not* apply. Here we should listen to the counsel of Teddy Roosevelt, "Walk softly and carry a big stick." It has been truly said that nobody ever wins a war, and this is certainly true among witches. There is plenty of prosperity, love, health and happiness to go around, so we need not try to steal it from each other—and the energy spent in a battle between aggressors causes much negative "fallout" for both for months. Thus the *passive defense* is best, and it is also most effective. When an attack *thoughtform* is built and sent to you, it is still attached to its maker. So if it cannot work its misery on you, it has nothing to do but to return to its maker, misery and all. When your constructive will is strong enough, you may capture a negative *thoughtform* and reprogram it for good—knowing that all energy is intrinsically good. Thus you wind up with an extra servant and the total amount of negativity in the world is decreased accordingly. This is a worthy ideal, but dangerous to all but the truly accomplished Witch. We will stay with the safer techniques proven effective through many centuries.

The Lemon Uncrossing Ritual

Rituals designed to break the power of negative spells are called *uncrossing rituals.* The Lemon Uncrossing Ritual is simple but very effective. Take a cup of salt, a fresh lemon and your athame (Witch's knife) to your altar. Light the white candles and protection incense, and anoint your brow, throat and heart with protection oil. Open the ritual with the Shiva Chant as we use it in the Basic Protection Ritual. Then put the lemon in the center of your altar and cut it into four slices (round slices, not quarters) with your athame, and chant:

> All spells against me, congregate,
>   Within this lemon, that's your fate.
> Sour spell to sour fruit,
>   You must go there 'cause it's your suit.
> Bound to this lemon evermore,
>   Each spell against me, that's your store.
> All in the lemon now I see,
>   And as my will, so mote it be!

When you feel that your chant has captured the negative *thoughtforms* in the lemon, begin to liberally sprinkle the lemon with salt as you chant:

Uncrossed! Uncrossed! This salt for me,
   Breaks up attacking energy.
Within this sour lemon bound,
   Now kills all spells with salt and sound.
As lemon dries in salt and air,
   I'm freed from harm and all despair.
Uncrossed and happy now, you see!
   And as my will, so mote it be.

Use plenty of salt, and when you feel that it is finished, conclude your ritual with thanks to all and the usual dismissal of the elementals. Leave the lemon near your altar where you can watch it. If it simply dries out as the weeks pass, your work is done, but if it should mildew the ritual must be repeated.

How Psychic Attacks from a Jealous Friend Were Handled

G.H. had sensed the barbs of psychic attack from a jealous friend for several days. The attack took the form of pains in the joints, particularly the arms and legs. G.H. was sure that a doctor would call her problem arthritis or bursitis, but she knew better. While casting about for psychic help, we suggested the lemon ritual. She reported, "The pain was so great I could barely walk, and my left wrist hurt so badly I had to stop knitting. But within one hour after completing the lemon ritual, my body was active and totally pain free. I also noticed that my 'friend' was quite subdued when I danced into the office the next morning. This is a wonderfully powerful ritual."

The Candle Uncrossing Ritual

The power of the candle is recognized throughout the occult, psychic, religious, and witchcraft worlds. And nowhere is the candle more useful than in breaking up negative spells and crossed conditions. For this work, obtain a "seven-day" candle in a jar. Department stores, drug stores, variety stores and many hardware stores carry the candles in glass jars about nine inches high and 2 1/2 inches in diameter. Select a candle with white wax in a clear jar for this ritual, don't be talked into the colored candles, they increase the danger to you but not the effectiveness of the ritual. You will also need an uncrossing oil. The best oil for this is made of equal parts of Sandalwood, Patchouli and Myrrh. To one dram of this mixture, add a drop of household ammonia and shake well. We will call this your uncrossing oil.

The beauty of this ritual is that its power continues to work for you with growing effectiveness for the whole time your candle continues to burn. This may be done in connection with the basic protection ritual, or as a short ritual all by itself. Write your name on a piece of white paper and put it under your candle. Pour a few drops of uncrossing oil into the top of your candle jar, light the candle, and chant:

> Fire and oil, now do your best,
>   Uncross and free me with great zest.
> Salamanders, Zephyrs, true,
>   Gnomes and Trolls, and Undines, too,
> Your mighty power works for me,
>   Uncrossing as you set me free.
> Success and power now to me,
>   And as my will, so mote it be!

How a Salesman Snapped Out of His Negative Psychic Attack

A young salesman, G.N., woke up one morning with a slight headache and a depressed feeling. He had a "lousy day" with no effectiveness on the job. By evening, G's body began to feel dull and listless while the headache persisted. He wondered if he was "coming down with something," but a little reflection convinced him that psychic attack was more likely. He used the candle ritual after dinner. Let's hear the results in his words: "Just as I finished the first chant of the candle ritual, I could *feel* the negative influences fading away. In less than fifteen minutes, I felt great! I always keep a spare candle and dram of uncrossing oil on hand now, just in case."

How to Plug the Chinks in Your Psychic Armor

Lasting protection and success requires that feeling of inner *worthiness* we talked about in the basic protection ritual and in the mirror ritual. If there is any doubt, review and re-use the mirror ritual until you can hold your head high with that inner knowing that you have made peace with yourself and so with the great forces and powers of nature.

We might also discuss the use of protective amulets and talismans, but we will go into detail on this extremely useful subject in our next chapter. Meanwhile, we will turn to a complete ritual for protection from the spells, curses and hexes of others.

Complete Ritual for Protection Against the Spells, Hexes, Curses and Psychic Attacks of Others

Preparation for the Ritual: Materials needed in addition to your normal altar set up are: (1) White candles for your altar candle holders (2) A white "Seven-day" candle in a clear glass jar (3) A dram of uncrossing oil (4) Your favorite protection oil (5) Protection incense (6) Your Witch's Cord and Athame (7) A fresh lemon (8) A cup of salt (9) Your chalice full of water and a spoon (10) The normal supply of matches, etc.

If possible, this ritual should be performed within the nine-foot circle. Using your Witch's cord and some masking tape, lay out a nine-foot circle, and a seven-foot circle each with the same center, and put your altar at the center of the two circles. Gather all your materials close to your altar, and the ceremony is ready to begin.

Ritual Step #1: Light your white altar candles, pick up your Athame and salute the candles with it. Walk to the east edge of your nine-foot circle and ritually draw it with the Athame, (Use the point of the Athame as if it were a piece of chalk with which you draw the circle) proceeding in a counter clockwise direction as you use the Shiva Chant:

> Lovely, powerful Shiva, God of sweeping change.
> > Sweep away the lesser, shut it out of range.
> Leave the beauty and the Light, bright and clean and fair.
> > Remove all vibrations of misery and despair.
> Leave this place and these fine things, fresh and bright and pure,
> > Holy as your own fine self, bright, complete and sure.
> Lovely, powerful Shiva, my thanks to you I give,
> > That from your sweeping power, in beauty may I live.

Ritual Step #2: Go back to your altar and put a spoon full of salt into your chalice of water. Stir it well. Then hold your hands over the mixture as you chant:

> Salt in water, by casting thee,
>   No spell nor unknown purpose be
> Except in true accord with me,
>   And as my will, so mote it be!

When you feel the mixture is well charged, pick up the chalice and walk to the east edge of your protective circle. (Never step outside of the circle once it is drawn, until the ritual is completed). Sprinkle the inside of your circle with the salt and water mixture as you repeat the chant, proceeding in a counter clockwise direction all the way around the circle.

Ritual Step #3: Return to your altar, replace the chalice and pick up your Athame. Again salute the candles, and proceed to the east edge of your seven-foot circle. Ritually draw the seven-foot circle with your Athame as you repeat the Shiva Chant.

Ritual Step #4: Return to your altar, replace the Athame, and pick up your chalice of salt and water. Proceed to the East edge of your seven-foot circle and sprinkle the inside of the circle with your salt mixture as you repeat the salt and water chant.

Ritual Step #5: Return to your altar, replace the chalice and light your incense from the right hand candle. Repeat the Fire Elemental Invocation:

> Creatures of fire, this charge I give,
>   No evil in my presence live,
> No phantom, spook, nor spell may stay
>   Around this place, not night nor day.
> Hear my will addressed to thee,
>   And as my word, so mote it be!

Ritual Step #6: Anoint all of your body's orifices, your brow, throat, and heart with the protection oil. Put a small drop of oil on your altar and chant:

> And now this oily essence fair
>   Adds its great power to the air,
> Attracting spirits of the Light,
>   Protecting me both day and night.
> This charge is true and proper, see,
>   And as my will, so mote it be!

Ritual Step #7: Put the lemon in the center of your altar, cut it into 4 slices with your Athamé, and chant:

> All spells against me, congregate,
>   Within this lemon, that's your fate.
> Sour spell to sour fruit,
>   You must go there 'cause it's your suit.
> Bound to this lemon evermore,
>   Each spell against me, that's your store.
> All in the lemon now I see,
>   And as my will, so mote it be!

When you feel that the negativity is captured in the lemon, sprinkle it liberally with salt as you chant:

> Uncrossed! Uncrossed! This salt for me,
>   Breaks up attacking energy.
> Within this sour lemon bound,
>   Now kills all spells with salt and sound.
> As lemon dries in salt and air,
>   I'm freed from harm and all despair.
> Uncrossed and happy now, you see!
>   And as my will, so mote it be!

Ritual Step #8: Pour some uncrossing oil into the top of your seven day candle. Light the candle and chant:

> Fire and oil now do your best,
>   Uncross and free me with great zest.
> Salamanders, Zephyrs, true,
>   Gnomes and Trolls, and Undines, too,
> Your mighty power works for me,
>   Uncrossing as you set me free.
> Success and power now to me,
>   And as my will, so mote it be!

Ritual Step #9: Enjoy a mood of peace, growth and safety as you chant:

> Spirit of the Great White Light,
>   Burn away my psychic night.
> Let me feel your loving care,

> Give me joy and love to share.
> Make of me your willing tool.
> Let fulfillment be my rule,
> That my growth may be a Light,
> Saving others from the night.

Close the ritual as always with thanks and the dismissal of the elementals:

> "I give my loving thanks to all the spirits and elementals who have participated here. And to the elementals, I dismiss you. Go about your appointed tasks and return to your native habitats, harming no one on the way. Blessed be."

Benefits of the Ritual

This is an excellent ritual to use when things seem to be in the doldrums, and particularly to break a long string of "bad luck." C.G. felt near the "end of his rope." His wife had left him and a messy divorce action was in process. Business had dropped way off, he seemed to have chronic stomach trouble, and to top it all off he had just been in an automobile accident. While musing about the feeling that, "Somebody up there hates me," he got the definite impression that he must be under psychic attack. He left work early to gather the materials and used the complete ritual for protection that night. Within three days he received a reasonable offer of a divorce settlement, new orders began to flow into his small business and the insurance company settled the automobile accident case. He suddenly found himself free of worry, so the stomach problem cleared right up and he launched a new and happy phase of his life. It will work for you, too, if the ritual is performed sincerely.

CHAPTER POINTS TO REMEMBER

1) Psychic control and attack takes many forms—from the simple frown when somebody disapproves of your actions to deliberate black magic.

2) You can learn to recognize attempts to control and/or attack you. Follow the procedure: Challenge all suggestions, examine all urges and negative feelings, and study all fleeting aches and pains

or runs of "bad luck." When you sense a psychic problem, react with a protective ritual.

3) Using the Home Protection Ritual on the night of the full moon will mightily help keep you free from robbery and vandalism.

4) Passive defense is best—avoid a battle of the Titans whenever possible.

5) For simple psychic attack the Lemon Uncrossing Ritual and/or the Candle Uncrossing Ritual will break the negative spell and release you to a naturally happy, productive life.

6) When things seem really bad, break out of the mess by using the Complete Ritual for Protection against the Spells, Hexes, Curses and Psychic Attacks, of Others.

Chapter Ten

How to Make and Use Amulets, Talismans and Charms for Protection, Mystic Powers and Good Luck

*H*ave you ever carried a rabbit's foot? A four leaf clover? A St. Christopher Medal? Did you ever hang a horseshoe over your door? If you spill salt, do you throw some over your left shoulder? How are you on walking under ladders? Grandma paid a lot more attention to these things than we "moderns" do, and any good Witch will tell you she was right. The purpose of this chapter is not to sell you a bunch of worn out supersititions, but to explore the protective and "lucky" powers of *things.* Just as candles, incense, herbs and oils add power to your rituals, so properly consecrated amulets, talismans and charms have power to influence the unseen side of life to your benefit.

Stones and Minerals for Protection and Good Fortune

The ancient science of Astrology relates the lucky and protective minerals to the sign under which you were born. Astrologers occasionally differ, but we will present a consensus based on our research and personal experience. You should consider your moon sign and rising sign of equal importance to the Sun sign and use the most appealing items. Let's look at it in table form and then discuss its value to *you:*

Date of Birth	Your Sun Sign	Lucky and Protective Stones and Minerals	Color
Mar 21/Apr 19	Aries	Diamond, Amethyst, Topaz, Garnet, Iron, Steel	Red

Apr 19/May 20	Taurus	Coral, Sapphire, Emerald, Turquoise, Agate, Zircon, Copper	Azure
May 20/Jun 21	Gemini	Aquamarine, Agate, Amber, Emerald, Topaz, Aluminum	ElectricBlue
Jun 21/Jul 22	Cancer	Opal, Pearl, Emerald, Moonstone, Silver	Pearl/Rose
Jul 22/Aug 22	Leo	Diamond, Ruby, Chrysoberyl, Sardonyx, Gold	Orange/Gold
Aug 22/Sep 23	Virgo	Jade, Rhodonite, Sapphire, Carnelian, Aluminum	Gray/Blue
Sep 23/Oct 23	Libra	Opal, Sapphire, Quartz, Jade, Turquoise, Copper	Pale Orange
Oct 23/Nov 22	Scorpio	Bloodstone, Aquamarine, Topaz, Jasper, Silver	Dark Red
Nov 22/Dec 21	Sagittarius	Lapis Lazuli, Topaz, Turquoise, Coral, Tin	Purple
Dec 21/Jan 20	Capricorn	Onyx, Jet, Ruby, Malachite, Lead	Brown
Jan 20/Feb 19	Aquarius	Aquamarine, Jade, Flourspar, Sapphire, Zircon, Aluminum	Green
Feb 19/Mar 21	Pisces	Amethyst, Alexandrite, Bloodstone, Stitchite, Silver	Ocean Blue

The astrological selection of a mineral or stone is a source of power but an equally important factor in your choice should be how the individual stone appeals to you. Your local lapidary or Curio shop might have a good variety of rough or tumbled stones from which to choose one that both suits you and "likes" you. We are in the planning stage of your personal Lucky Meditation Stone, so care in the selection will pay big dividends. The size of your stone is a blending of personal taste and utility—it should be suitable for traveling in your pocket or purse, or nestling in a lady's brassiere. Let's finish the selection and consecration process before we discuss the many practical uses.

When you have located a group of stones of the variety and price that appeals to you, the selection process is much like picking the right melon in a grocery store. Pass your left hand slowly over the group of stones and feel for a flow of warm energy. In almost any group of stones, one or more will respond to you. Choose the stone that generates the greatest amount of friendly energy flow—this is the compatibility between *Witch* and *stone* that we can use to your great advantage.

How to Consecrate and Use Your Lucky Meditation Stone

The consecration ceremony is designed to amplify the naturally existing "love affair" between you and your chosen personal stone. Use protection incense and white candles with the basic protection ritual. When the mood is well set, rub your stone with exorcism oil as you chant:

> Stone of beauty, fine to see,
>   Be consecrated now to me.
> Partners now in growth and life,
>   Helping well in time of strife.
> Tensions strong you take for me,
>   Bring good luck effectively.
> Great amulet for me you'll be,
>   And as my will, so mote it be!

When your ritual is complete, you have produced much more than a mere lucky piece. An original idea was the passing of the human's tensions to the Lucky Meditation Stone as a preliminary step to meditation, but this was quickly expanded to using the stone to absorb your tensions at any time or place.

How to Transfer Your Tensions
to Your Lucky Meditation Stone

You have consecrated the stone and bound it into your personal program of evolution. Thus you gave it the desire to absorb the tensions and pressures of life that might otherwise be harmful to your body. There remains only the regular giving of opportunity to your stone by use. Keep it with you, in a pocket or purse, always. The. more you let it feel that it is a partner in your progress, the more positive help it will give you. The process of transfering your tensions is so simple that it can be done in public without drawing undue attention. Simply hold the stone in your hand (in both hands if possible, but one will do), take a reasonably deep breath and visualize all your tensions and pressures flowing through your hand into the rock. Know that the stone can take a lot more pressure than your delicate human organism, and it will serve you happily and painlessly as often as you *let* it.

How Melissa Used Her Stone to Relieve Her Tensions

Melissa S. had developed a skin rash that the doctor told her was caused by nervous tension. Melissa went to a rock shop and bought a lovely piece of tumbled turquoise. It projected a strong flow of warm energy to her hand to make the selection process easy, and the consecration ritual seemed especially pleasant to her. This is her report after a month of using the stone: "That lovely little stone is priceless! I don't know how I got along without it. I wear it in my brassiere, close to my heart. And whenever I even start to get tense, the stone gets hot to remind me that it will take my pressure. Then I just put my left hand casually over the stone and take a deeper than normal breath. When the stone has taken my tension it feels cool again. This is almost unbelievable! I'm off the tranquilizers, my skin is clear and lovely, and life is beautiful again!"

How to Program Your Subconscious
with Your Lucky Meditation Stone

If your stone is reasonably small and flat, it can be used to stimulate the creativity and problem-solving ability of your subconscious mind. This technique is highly effective.

Bring your stone and a roll of scotch tape to the altar for your bedtime ritual. Just before you end the ritual, use a short piece of scotch tape to attach the stone to the middle of your forehead. Address your reflection in the altar mirror as if it were your subconscious mind, and instruct it: "This stone placed upon our forehead is your reminder of your work for tonight. While the body is asleep, your assignment is to bring the creative solution to our problem of _(whatever it is)_ . When you are ready, wake the body long enough for me to write down the solution, then put it back into a restful, regenerative sleep. Your cooperation will make life more comfortable for the entire organism, and thus for you, too. Do it."

Then be sure that there is a pad of paper and a pencil on the nightstand within easy reach from the bed. When your ritual work is concluded, go off to a restful sleep confident that your answer will be brought to you. *Be sure to follow through* when you are awakened with the answer. Write down enough to clearly remember it in the morning. Without the taking of notes, you will suffer the disappointment of realizing that you had the answer last night, but forgot it. Failure to follow through will weaken the contact with your subconscious mind and cause it to be less apt to cooperate, so exercise your constructive will with this ritual and *make those notes, regardless of the hour or how much you would prefer to stay asleep!*

How a Problem of Unemployment Was Solved

Harry N. was given his layoff notice from the junior engineering position he had held for just over a year. There was a brief feeling of despair before he decided to use the technique of programming his subconscious for help. He wasn't quite sure what to ask for, so he kept the instruction general: "Bring me the creative solution to this employment problem."

During the early hours of the morning, Harry awakened long enough to sketch an electronic circuit that proved to be an improvement over a subsystem that his ex-employer used in considerable quantity. An enthusiastic trip to the purchasing department convinced the company of significant savings by buying from Harry. And this was the beginning of a successful new electronics firm.

How to Harness the Witchcraft Power of Jewelry

All precious and semi-precious stones have power as well as beauty, thus the successful Witch will often wear a greater than average amount of jewelry. When selecting a new piece for your collection, the Birthstone suggested by astrology is a good guide, but you may find you're attracted to the stone of your Moon sign or Rising Sign for power as great as the Sun Sign (see also the final section of this chapter for selection of metals and stones). Your personal taste is important also, but as in the meditation stone selection the interaction between you and the individual piece of jewelry as shown by the energy flow to your hand is most important.

Although the best ritual work is performed while the body is quite nude, jewelry is an exception. Well selected and consecrated jewelry adds power to your ritual work and *thoughtform* creation by the presence of its essence in your aura. The first introduction of jewelry into your ritual work should be the consecration ceremony. Use the Altar Consecration Ritual as given in Chapter 2. At the point where you would consecrate the altar, substitute the jewelry consecration. Anoint your ring, necklace, broach or bracelet with exorcism oil and chant:

> Jewel(s) of beauty, picked for me,
>   Consecrated now you'll be.
> Be ye bound to me in Light,
>   Ever keep my aura bright.
> Funnel in fresh energy,
>   Power all my spells for me.
> Happy partners now are we.
>   As my will, so mote it be.

Just wearing a piece of consecrated jewelry during your rituals will add power, but when you can work it into the energy producing part of your *thoughtform* building work, the results are often spectacular.

W.O.'s report speaks for itself. Let's take it in her own words: "My ritual work seemed a bit bogged down on two big projects, so I poked around in my jewelry box and found a nice ruby ring that I hadn't worn for a while. I consecrated that and the sapphire I have worn for years. Just before my ritual, I put one ring on each hand and turned them around so the stones were on the palm side of my hands. I felt a considerably stronger energy flow at *thoughtform* building time, and it proved to be just the margin of victory. During the first week I brought about the settlement of my two year old accident claim (and I considered it a good settlement, too), and the following week my new perfect husband *thoughtform* brought in an extremely promising candidate"!

Now you know why Witches appear to wear a greater amount of jewelry than so-called normal people.

The Ankh and How It Protects You

The *Ankh* or *Crux Ansata* has been a symbol of life and protection since before the dawn of recorded history. In the ancient occult traditions, the ankh was brought to Egypt's Inner Temples from Atlantis, but we are most interested in its usefulness to *you* today. Worn on a ring or on a chain around your neck, the ankh is a powerful talisman for warding off "evil" and defending you against the negative suggestions and spells of others. Silver is the best material for the protective use, but the ankh is available today in a great multiplicity of sizes and materials including silver, gold, wood, bronze, copper, and even lead. Taking your astrological metals into account, you would still make your final selection of an ankh by passing your left hand over several and picking the one which responds to you with the greatest energy flow. The consecration ritual is performed as for other jewelry except that there is a special ankh consecration chant:

> Ankh of power, sign of life,
>> Protect me evermore from strife.
> Bound to me by word and Light,
>> Keep me safe both day and night.
> A strong protector unto me,
>> And as my will, so mote it be!

If someone asks to see your ankh after it has been consecrated to you, the proper answer is: "I'm sorry, but I may not take if off." Such is the power of the tradition that a good Witch will not "take a chance" of being unprotected even for a few moments. And if any other person handled your ankh, it is good policy to have a fresh consecration for it as soon as possible.

How a Negative Spell Was Broken

For over a year H.S. wondered if he had been "cursed or something." Nothing seemed to go right—he lost three different jobs, his girl friend discarded him, and "even the neighborhood dogs that used to be friendly took to snarling at me." He used the Complete Ritual for Protection against the Spells of Others (as in Chapter 9) and followed up by consecrating a small ankh to wear on a chain around his neck. His report: "Whatever it was, the negative spell is broken! I was called back to my old job with a nice raise. I have a lovely new girl friend and we're very close to marriage. And those dogs that used to snarl at me are all tail-waggers again"!

How to Harness the Talismanic Value of the Square of Saturn

From the time of the great King Solomon, the Square of Saturn has been used in magic and witchcraft for protection from all adversaries in corporeal or entity form. The square is even more effective when used in its proper place as part of the Second Pentacle of Saturn. This is the way Solomon himself used it. Figure 1 shows the complete Pentacle. This is most effective when reproduced in *black* ink on virgin parchment, though some find it easier to wear when engraved on a disk of silver.

The "do it yourself" work of making your own will add more power to your pentacles than genuine virgin parchment—for most work a good grade of rag bond will be excellent. We might anticipate the next section sufficiently to suggest that your Square of Saturn Pentacle will make one side of a very important talisman to wear around your neck on a chain or ribbon. Thus choice of a standard size (2 1/2 to 3 inches in diameter) will make it easier to use your pentacles in combination or as medallions.

The *Square of Saturn*, itself, is:

S	A	T	O	R
A	R	E	P	O
T	E	N	E	T
O	P	E	R	A
R	O	T	A	S

Part of the magic of the square is its perfection of form that reads the same from any direction, and more comes from the Kabbalistic Numerology. Set in the Pentacle (see Figure 1)

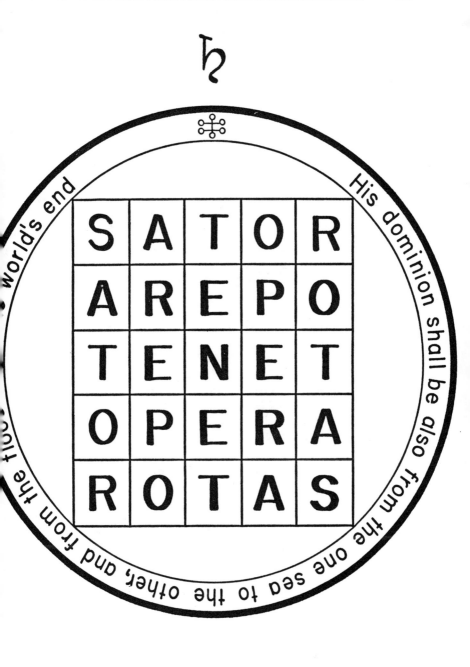

Figure 1
The Square of Saturn as Part of the Pentacle of Saturn

and properly consecrated, this becomes an exceptionally good protector. The total equipment necessary to make your pentacle is a compass, a straight edge and a pen with black ink. The vibrations from *you* during your loving construction help bind it to you— thus your mood of confidence and peace is essential during the time you are doing your drawing and lettering work. Be neat, but not a perfectionist. This will be a *one of a kind* pentacle because you put yourself into it, even to the uneven lettering. The pentacle should be carefully glued to a wooden or metal disk and protected with several coats of clear varnish. Then it can be consecrated with a ritual similar to the ankh consecration. Here the chant is:

> Square of power, Saturn's life,
>> Protect me ever more from strife.
> Bound to me by word and Light,
>> Keep me safe both day and night.
> A strong protector unto me,
>> And as my will, so mote it be!

Now let's put Jupiter on the other side of your medallion to bring riches, honor and wealth.

A Jupiter Talisman to Attract Riches, Honor and Wealth

Figure 2 sets forth the Fourth Pentacle of Jupiter. After the experience of making your Saturn Pentacle, this one will be easy. Your Jupiter Pentacle should be made with bright blue ink. When it is finished, glue it to the other side of your medallion and protect it with several coats of clear varnish. Consecrate this side to Jupiter with a ritual as for the ankh, but using this chant:

> Mighty Jupiter, bound to me by pentacle of blue,
>> Expansion great do bring to me, wealth and riches, **too.**
> Adoniel and Bariel watch lovingly o'er me.
>> In your good hands I place my lot, thanks and so mote it be!

Your Saturn/Jupiter Medallion may be worn on a silver chain or a necklace braided from strands of black and bright blue ribbon. This makes a wonderfully effective combination of protection and opulence. R.S. reported that he used black and blue marking pens to make the two pentacles. He glued them to a circular piece he

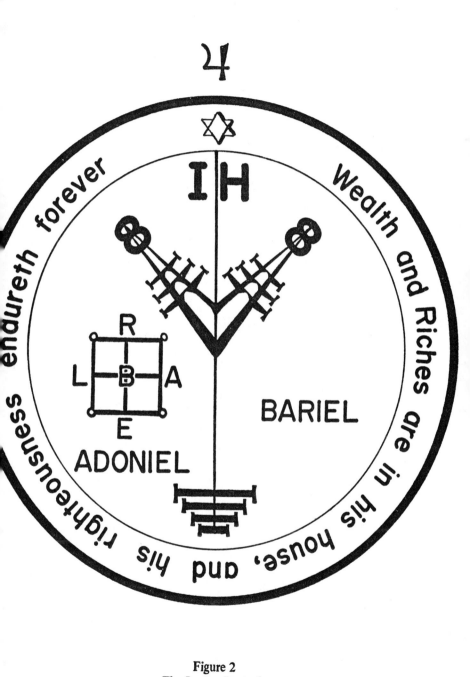

Figure 2
The Jupiter Pentacle

cut from an aluminum can and protected it with varnish from a small spray can. The total cost of the project was $1.85 and about two hours time. Here is his happy report: "During the first two weeks after I finished my Saturn/Jupiter Medallion an annoying wart dropped off the back of my hand leaving no trace of its past presence, I won three different $50 football pools, and I got a completely unexpected 25¢ an hour raise. To anyone who might suggest 'coincidence' just tell them thanks, but I'll keep my medallion."

How to Attract Power, Honor and Love with a Venus/Mars Pentacle Medallion

The construction technique is the same for this medallion as for the Saturn/Jupiter one. Figure 3 gives you the Venus Pentacle— this should be done in a bright green color. Figure 4 is the Mars Pentacle which should be done in bright red. If you prefer a braided necklace to a silver chain, let the colors of the ribbon be red and green. This medallion can be finished and consecrated as one unit. Use the consecration ritual as for the ankh, and chant:

>Male and female, Venus, Mars,
>   The ancient power of the stars
>Is bound to me by green and red,
>   The laurel wreath is for my head.
>Fame and honor, power, love,
>   Rain down upon me from above.
>Mars and Venus bound to me,
>   And as my will, so mote it be!

When Sheri Y. consecrated her Venus/Mars Medallion, she received a phone call that same evening. It was a gentleman she had been hoping to meet for more than a month. He asked for a date to take her to a very exclusive party—two dreams came true with one happy phone call! And the power of the medallion has lasted through courtship and a happy marriage.

How to Design Your Own Special Purpose Amulet

Because we are each uniquely individual, there is not an all inclusive amulet or group of amulets. So perhaps the best offering

Figure 3
The Venus Pentacle

Figure 4
The Mars Pentacle

we can give you is a set of ideas from which you can design the special amulet most suited to you.

How to choose the metal for your amulet: The different metals have their own special properties of attraction which should be considered before choosing the stones:

> *Aluminum* attracts mental alertness, invention and the art of making money. It helps you to be practical and think quickly. It is particularly suited for the signs of Gemini, Virgo and Aquarius.
>
> *Copper* is warm and earthy. It is a guardian of health, considered especially protective against arthritis and rheumatism. It is protective also against depression and negative thoughts or entities. The Astrological association is particularly good for Taurus and Libra.
>
> *Gold* attracts success in monetary matters and the theater. It is the king of metals and is associated with leaders in any field. Its natural Astrological sign is Leo.
>
> *Iron* is the metal of weaponry, of attack and defense—war. It is associated with Mars and particularly the sign of Aries.
>
> *Lead* is heavy and serious but mystical. It is associated with Saturn, the teacher and task master. It is good for breaking spells and for protection against flamboyant people. Lead is especially associated with the sign of Capricorn.
>
> *Silver* is the metal of dreams and receptivity. It is good for protecting secrets and keeping you safe on the water. It is female, just as gold is male. There is a strong emotional quality to silver that makes it ideally suited to projecting thoughts and moods. It is associated with the signs of Cancer, Pisces and Scorpio.
>
> *Tin* is the metal of luck and good fortune, progress and expansion. It is associated with Jupiter and so with Sagittarius.

How to choose stones for your amulet: Whether you plan a ring, broach, pendant bracelet or necklace for your amulet, the mixing of stones to attract the forces you need is effective. With the right metal or metals and stones, the accomplished witch can work tremendous feats of healing, love, prosperity and power. Pick your stones for their qualities:

> *Agate* attracts peace, victory in games, happiness and good luck. It is especially good for the signs of Gemini and Taurus.
>
> *Amethyst* attracts love and good luck and is a protector against sorcery. It is best when used by an Aries or Aquarius.
>
> *Beryl* is for deep romance and love. It brings hope and protects against the fascinations and spells of witchcraft.

Bloodstone is also known as Carnelian. It is said to bring friendship, to calm people and soothe flaring tempers, and is protection against the evil eye and depression. It is strongest when used by those ruled by Pisces, Scorpio and Virgo.

Coral is one of the strongest of the protective stones. It protects against the evil eye, all spells, natural disasters and unfortunate occurrences. It is associated with the planet Venus and is especially powerful when used by those of the signs of Taurus, Sagittarius or Libra.

Diamond attracts power, riches and friends. It is believed excellent for reconciling differences between friends who have quarreled. It symbolizes peace, fidelity and opulence, and is strongest when used by those of the signs Leo and Aries.

Emerald is a stone of precognition and the ability to see into the future. It nurtures love and beauty and turns negative spells back upon the sender. It is most powerful when used by those of the signs of Taurus, Gemini and Cancer.

Garnet attracts purity, sincerity and understanding. It tends to be a bit stuffy and Victorian but is quite useful to the signs of Aquarius and Capricorn.

Jasper protects from pain and guards one's independence. It brings good fortune and protection from the controlling influences of others. It is most useful for the signs of Virgo and Sagittarius.

Jade has been a sacred stone for centuries on end, bringing good luck, protection from disease or evil spirits and enhancing one's occult powers. It represents serenity and immortality, and is powerful for the signs of Libra, Aquarius and Virgo.

Lapis Lazuli is an attractor of powerful and highly evolved spirits. Its possessor is believed to be endowed with great supernatural powers. It is most powerful when used by those of the sign Sagittarius.

Moonstone is the stone of love. It protects love and inspires the tender passions. It is especially powerful when carried by those of the sign Cancer.

Opal is a dangerous stone for those not in tune with it. It is mystical in nature and brings good luck and extra mental powers to those of Libra, Cancer and Scorpio. If you are of any other sign, experiment with opals very carefully.

Ruby is a stone of power, loyalty and courage. It is a focuser of occult energy and protector from trouble as well as an aid in love and passion. It is most powerful when used by those of Cancer, Capricorn or Leo.

Sapphire is a stone of witchcraft and occult power, but it radiates gentleness and peace. It is good for bringing justice and truth to light and is powerful for those of Taurus, Virgo, Libra and Aquarius.

Sardonyx is a protector against spells and incantations. It sharpens the wits of the wearer and imparts both warmth and precision. It is strongest for those of Leo and Virgo.

Topaz is a protector of warriors. It puts demons to flight and vanquishes the spells of sorcerors. It is used for divining purposes to locate both water and treasure. It is most powerful for those of the signs of Scorpio, Aries, Gemini and Sagittarius.

Turquoise brings love and courage and is a protector against violence of thought or deed. It is good for reducing bodily or mental tensions and is strongest for those of the sign of Sagittarius, Taurus and Libra.

Zircon attracts fame and fortune. It is considered a wishing stone as well as a protector against accidents or natural disasters. It is strongest for Taurus and Aquarius.

Within your price range and taste, you will find plenty of room to express your individuality in amulets. When you have completed the consecration ceremony for yours (as for other jewelry) it is ready to take its place as a powerful tool in your arsenal of Witchcraft.

CHAPTER POINTS TO REMEMBER

1) Your "Lucky Meditation Stone" will have great value to you. Choose one that is lovely in appearance and compatible in vibration both to your sense of energy flow and your astrological sign.

2) After it is consecrated, practice transferring your tensions to your meditation stone. You will find improved health and peace of mind as a result.

3) your meditation stone can also be used to program your subconscious mind for problem solving and creativity of all kinds.

4) Your present jewelry can be harnessed to enhance your powers of Witchcraft. Consecrate it and use it in all your ceremonial and spell casting work.

5) Powerful protection is available from a consecrated ankh or a medallion of pentacles of Saturn and Jupiter.

6) The Venus/Mars Medallion will add much power to your love making and business activities.

7) You can design and consecrate your unique amulet for your most cherished purpose. Within the descriptions of the stones and metals lies the combination of power for you. Try your hand and experience *success.*

Chapter Eleven

How to Use Rituals to Gain
Power Over Other People

Does some person intimidate you? Feel pushed around? Or just ignored? Would you like to be known as dynamic, forceful, and effective? There is no reason to let people and life continue to push you around—you can begin to assert your freedom and power now! We will begin with a series of three rituals of increasing power. Let's caution you to use only the amount of power you need in any individual case. Always try the first ritual before deciding you need the second, and use the first two before you would think of trying the third.

Ritual to Calm an Angry Person

If a person close to you is angry, either at you or the world in general, you can make your life more comfortable by helping him (or her) to turn loose of the grudge and become human again. This can be an extension of the basic protection ritual. In addition to the normal altar supplies (including *white* candles) you will need an herb mixture made of equal parts of passion flowers and orris powder carefully blended in your mortar and pestle, and a ceramic dish (or a thurible) in which to burn it. Before you begin your ritual, make a small mound of your herb mixture on the dish and place it on your altar. Then write the person's name on a small piece of white paper, leave it on the altar and your ritual is ready to begin. When you reach the end of the basic protection ritual, light the piece of paper (with the person's name on it) from a candle and use the paper to ignite the herb mixture. Then chant:

Peace and love I send to thee.
No longer angry shall you be.

148

In peace we live eternally,
And as my will, so mote it be!

Repeat the chant three, seven, or nine times, and use the ritual for three consecutive nights. If possible, start the ritual on the first Saturday after a full moon, but any day or night will do in an emergency.

Marie Q. seemed to have a running feud with the girl on the next machine in the laboratory where they both worked. The other girl constantly snapped at Marie and seemed to go out of her way to make life on the job uncomfortable. On Friday night, after a particularly miserable week, Marie decided to try the Ritual to Calm an Angry Person on the girl at work. She used the ritual Friday, Saturday and Sunday evenings. On Monday morning Marie went to work with hope for a better time. She met the "antagonist" with a friendly smile and was almost surprised to have it returned in kind. The girl asked Marie to eat with her at lunch time, and they have become fast friends. I hope that *you* never need this ritual, but if you do, it is there to help you.

Ritual to Destroy Your Enemy's Power to Harm You

What happens if you have used the Ritual to Calm an Angry Person three or more consecutive nights, but relations have not improved and the person seems to be really "out to get you?" Let's say again that this Ritual to Destroy Your Enemy's Power to Harm You should be attempted only after giving the first ritual a good chance.

This time we make a mixture of two parts Sandalwood Powder to one part Bay Leaves and one part Dill Seed. Mix it well in your mortar and pestle until it is smooth and fine like a powdered incense. Make a good sized mound of the mixture on a ceramic dish (or your Thurible) as you would with any powdered incense. Write your enemy's name on a small piece of white paper and take this and the herb incense to your altar along with the normal supplies for your basic protection ritual. When you reach the end of the ritual, light the paper with your enemy's name on it from a candle, and use it to light the herb incense. Then chant:

As this incense burns away,
(Name of enemy)'s power fades today,

No longer causing me alarm,
   Nevermore able me to harm.
Immune to spells forever me,
   And as my will, so mote it be!

Use the chant nine times, then conclude your ritual as usual. The ritual is most effective when started on a Saturday night during the dark of the moon, and continued for seven consecutive nights. When using this and the previous ritual in tandem, the timing is just right. There are always two Saturdays between the full moon and the next new moon. Thus you can use the Ritual to Calm an Angry Person for three days beginning with the first Saturday and there are four days to determine if you need to use the Ritual to Destroy an Enemy's Power to Harm You on the following Saturday.

How a Mother Overcame Psychic Attacks

Mrs. Sharon D. discovered that her 19-year-old son, Wally, had started keeping company with a young girl of "very questionable morals." When Sharon tried to talk Wally into breaking off the relationship with the girl we will call Susie, he innocently told Susie about it.

Then the trouble started for Sharon! All manner of ridiculous things seemed to happen to her—dishes would literally break in her hands, she had five flat tires in two weeks (the tires were almost brand new!), and the people on her job became hostile where before they had been most cordial.

But worse from Sharon's viewpoint, Wally moved in to live with Susie and refused to come around his mother. It took almost a week for Sharon to figure out that it was not coincidence but psychic attack. It was on the night of the full moon when a glass broke in her hand and cut her finger that Sharon decided action was necessary. The next day was Saturday, so she used the ritual to calm an angry person—doing it twice, once for Susie and once for Wally. She repeated the ritual for three nights, but the attacking manifestations continued throughout the week.

The following Saturday, Sharon began the seven day ritual to destroy Susie's power to harm her. As the week progressed, the manifestations of attack slowly subsided—after the seventh performance of the ritual Sharon's life returned to normal, and less than a week later Wally broke up with Susie and apologized to his mother. One wonders at the difference if Sharon had not used the defensive rituals in time!

Ritual to Drive Away Troublesome People

We opened this chapter by cautioning you to use the more powerful rituals only after finding that the safer rituals of less power are clearly not sufficient to your needs. There is a very sound reason for this—when you set the energy in motion, it must do something. If your adversary is well-protected, the whole bit may come back to you! Take careful inventory of the side effects from using the first rituals to be sure you can handle this one, otherwise *you* may be the one uprooted.

For this ritual you will need to prepare a special herb incense consisting of:

1/4 oz. Jalop powder	1/4 oz. Rosemary
1/4 oz. Snakehead	1/4 oz. Charcoal
1/16 oz. Brimstone	1/16 oz. Ginger

Feel the power flowing from your hands and eyes as you thoroughly mix the incense in your mortar and pestle. This ceremony is best performed as part of the Complete Ritual for Protection Against the Spells of Others (see Chapter 9). Here you are working within the protection of the nine and seven foot circles. Along with the supplies for the basic ritual, you will need the special herb incense and a piece of burning charcoal. The ritual should be started at 7:01 p.m. on a Saturday while the moon is waning, and it is to be repeated at the same time for nine consecutive nights. When the protection ritual is finished, sprinkle your special herb incense upon the burning charcoal and use this chant nine times:

> In the Name of Azazel, I command that (name of the person) shall be compelled to leave my environment and that I may see him (or her) no more. As my will, so mote it be!

Take extra care to dismiss the elementals at the conclusion of the ceremony. Joe and Mary N. lived in a nice apartment for several years when a family of undesirables moved in above them. Mary tried talking to the wife to reduce the many annoyances from this family but there was no improvement. Joe talked to the landlord, but no help was forthcoming from there, either. Joe and Mary wondered if they had somehow antagonized the family when they had first moved in, so they tried the ritual to calm an angry person, but again there was no improvement. Thus to Joe and Mary it became a case of "It's either them or us." They decided to start properly, just after 7:00 o'clock on Saturday in the dark of the moon. It was a bit of a sacrifice for them because several of their favorite television programs came on at 7:00 o'clock during the week, but they kept up the ritual work for the full nine days. Three days later the family above abruptly moved out—there was no explanation and Joe and Mary never asked for one. . . . Their ritual work accomplished what they wanted. In a similar manner, you too can control actions of others to your benefit.

Ritual to Obtain Favor in Court

We all tend to get a bit nervous when we have to go to court. And although justice is theoretically impartial, it gives one great comfort to know that the unseen forces of Witchcraft are working in your favor. Consecrate a dark place large enough to hold a pint bottle. Three days before your scheduled court appearance, put 1/4 oz of jalop powder and 3/4 oz. of snake head into a pint bottle of water. Put the bottle in the consecrated place and chant over it:

> Saturn, Jupiter, Mercury, Mars,
>   Odin, Shiva, Agni, Thor,
> My day in court be you with me,
>   Victory swift and sure to see
> Your power great be on my side,
>   Opponents from the Light must hide.
> Victory is our certainty,
>   And as my will, so mote it be!

Repeat the chanting each evening and morning. Then on the morning of the court date, pour the mixture out your front door where you must walk through it as you leave the house. Carry a large piece of John the Conqueror Root in your pocket to the courtroom and know that you will win!

How a Ritual Helped Produce a Favorable Court Decision

It is helpful to combine this ritual with the Ritual to Destroy your Enemy's Power to Harm You. Together they guard you against treachery and open the mind of the judge and jury to your logical position. For years California law was notorious for favoring women in divorce cases, so I considered this report from Mr. J.A. an outstanding demonstration of the power of White Witchcraft: "My divorce case had dragged on for almost two years with nothing but aggravation and confusion. The lawyers were unable to work out a property settlement, so at long last a court date was set to let the judge do it. For the three days before, I used the Ritual to Obtain Favor in Court along with the Ritual to Destroy My Enemy's Power to Harm Me. I received a very fair hearing and a settlement that was much better than I dared hope for. Even the opposing attorney who had been most difficult in the past appeared cooperative and almost helpful. My ex-wife is provided for, but it was not the disaster predicted by so many of my friends who have been through it. I'm happy and *free!*"

How to Keep Your Husband (or Wife) at Home—
(Spell to Bind a Loved One to You)

Is the romance slipping out of your relationship? Have a sneaky feeling that your lover is looking around, or playing around already? Always the first step should be to look at yourself—are you still full of magic? How long has it been since you have given your lover a happy surprise? Work on your appearance and disposition, too. Then you are ready for the extra help of Witchcraft. Prepare for the Complete Love Attracting Ritual (as in Chapter 6), and take along a picture of your lover, a piece of brown wrapping paper and some spikenard (herb) when you go to your altar. Go through the complete ritual except for the conclusion itself. Then put your lover's picture face up on the brown paper in the center of your altar. Anoint the picture with your love oil and sprinkle it with the spikenard as you chant:

> Lover mine, be bound to me
> With limitless fidelity.

You're mine through all eternity,
And as my will, so mote it be!

Wrap the picture in the brown paper and bury it close to the house or in a large flower pot, repeating the chant as you cover it up. Sprinkle spikenard and a few drops of love oil on the surface of the dirt and chant again. Then conclude your ritual as usual.

How the Ritual Reclaimed a Husband's Love

Lenore Y. had been married seven years when her husband, Nate, seemed to get the "seven year itch." When he didn't react to her new hairdo and that slinky new negligee, she knew she was in real trouble. So Lenore decided that she must use the Spell to Bind a Loved One to You. Since they lived in a high-rise apartment, a flower pot was the only possible place to bury the picture. Lenore waited for a night when one of those phone calls told her she would be alone. She took a wallet size snapshot of Nate to the altar and enjoyed making her ritual richly elaborate. Two nights later, Nate came home with a bouquet of flowers. He confessed that he had been having an affair with a girl from his office and guaranteed that he had broken it off for all time. Lenore accepted his sincere apology and they entered a time of new marital happiness.

Ritual for Favorable Treatment of Your Letter

Often we find it necessary to use the mails to apply for a new job, sell a manuscript, or keep in touch with a loved one. One thing we all want is *response,* and of course the more favorable, the better. To help your letter, make a mixture of three parts jalop powder and one part basil. Take the herb mixture and your letter to your altar. Begin with the basic protection ritual, then sprinkle your letter lightly with the herb mixture as you chant:

Herb of power, do what's right.
Speed this letter in its flight.
Make the answer come to me
Quickly and successfully.
My hearty thanks I give to thee,
And as my will, so mote it be!

Seal the letter, conclude the ritual and mail the letter while the moon is in the sign of Gemini, or between seven and eight a.m. on any Wednesday.

For a hobby, S.A., writes humorous short verses. She had one very good verse that kept getting rejection notices, "for no good reason." One day S.A. decided to try the Ritual for Favorable Treatment of a Letter, "just to see if it might help." This time the verse was accepted. Let's continue in her own words: "Naturally I dismissed the first acceptance as coincidence—after all it was a good verse. But I decided to keep using the ritual and to keep score. In the past my rejection rate has averaged 80 percent. Since the use of the ritual the rate has dropped to less than 60 percent. That's enough to convince me."

Ritual for Acceptance by a New Group

Moving to a new town? Thinking of changing jobs? Is there a club or organization you'd like to join? Would you like to insure your acceptance in the new situation, or just make people in general more receptive to you? This is one of the great strengths of White Witchcraft. Prepare as for the complete love attracting ritual, but plan for a prosperity incense and a sachet composed of equal parts of jalop powder, vervain, snakehead and violet flowers. Use the chants and ritual for love attraction to the point of preparation of the sachet. Here you fill the sachet with the herb mixture (about 1/2 oz. total) as you chant:

> Acceptance is the keynote here,
>> My word is spoken loud and clear.
> All spirits of the Light be told
>> To charge my aura, make it bold.
> Let it open the hearts of all
>> Who come near me, both great and small.
> With Light and friendship magnetize
>> My being that all hearts shall rise
> To welcome me with friendship dear
>> And want to feel my presence near.
> My words to all who hear, a charm,
>> My smile dispelling all alarm,
> All doors shall open wide to me,
>> And as my will, so mote it be!

Close the ritual and dismiss the elementals as usual. Then carry the sachet on your person to each new place. If letters of application are involved, be sure to use the Ritual for Favorable Treatment of Your Letter before you mail them.

How a Prosperity Ritual Resulted in Many Job Offers

Charlie S., a middle-aged engineer caught in the aerospace layoff squeeze, had been unsuccessfully seeking a job for six months. He constantly answered ads with a good resume and was out "knocking on doors" regularly. Finally Charlie turned to Witchcraft. He used a complete prosperity ritual, and began to use the Ritual for Favorable Treatment of Your Letter with each resume he submitted. Suddenly there were three job interviews scheduled for one week. Charlie used the Ritual for Acceptance before going to each interview, and had the pleasure of choosing between three job offers. You could never tell Charlie that this was coincidence!

Complete Ritual for Building Personal Power

The altar supplies for this ritual include red candles, a power oil (one part Frankessence and one part Citron), Psychic Phenomena incense (see recipe in Chapter 3), your chalice of salt and water, and your normal altar accessories. This ritual is most effective when used on a Sunday or Thursday after a new moon. Set your time carefully to avoid interruptions, go to your altar and begin:

Ritual Step #1: Greet yourself and your spirit friends with a friendly smile. Mentally reach for the warmth and protection of the sphere of Light you build around yourself as you chant:

> Rama, Agni, Send the Light to me.
>> Rama, Agni, send the Light of power to me.
> Power to my aura give,
>> Bring through me the joy to live.
> Rama, Agni, send the Light that sets me free.

Ritual Step #2: Light your candles and incense, and chant:

> Creatures of fire, this charge to thee,
>> A thing of power I shall be.
> My word of power all shall bind,

> T'ward me all thoughts shall be most kind.
> Hear my word addressed to thee,
>> And as my will, so mote it be.

Ritual Step #3: Sprinkle the salt water liberally around your altar area as you chant:

> Salt and water, power to thee
>> Make this place both bright and free.
> All power safely keep for me.
> And as my will, so mote it be.

Ritual Step #4: Anoint your brow, heart and solar plexus with your power oil as you chant:

> And now this oily essence fair
>> Attracts great power from the air.
> Spirits of power stay with me,
>> A strong influence we shall be.
> This charge is true and proper, see.
>> And as my will, so mote it be!

Ritual Step #5: Now we are ready to build your real power *thoughtform.* Hold out your hands, and start the energy flowing as you have learned. Feed the growing *thoughtform* with love from your heart and power from your throat, eyes and brow as you chant:

> Form of power, built by me,
>> Filled with vital energy,
> Expand and grow that you may be
>> Bright enough for all to see.
> Extend my power far and wide,
>> Whome're you touch be on my side.
> Fame, acceptance, open doors,
>> We earn together more and more.
> All creatures like to have us near,
>> Old enemies now call us, dear.
> Success that's bright for all to see,
>> And as my will, so mote it be!

Ritual Step #6: Close the ritual with thanks to all and dismissal of the elementals.

How a Timid Person Suddenly Achieved Personal Power

A.L. had been considered a bit on the "mousy" side for years. When she used the Complete Ritual for Building Personal Power, it gave her a strong urge to get a new hairdo and a few stylish pieces of clothing. The *thoughtform* and the new appearance teamed up to make a whole new life style for A.L. as she reported: "For thirty-nine years my life could be described with one word, anonymity. Nobody ever notices me! After the ritual I got a strange urge to fix my hair and style up my wardrobe. The results are unbelievable! I have never held an office of any kind before, but I was just elected president of my social club. I got a sudden and unexpected promotion on my job. All sorts of men are flirting with me, and life is just full of happy surprises! I'll be using that ritual often to be sure that things keep up."

CHAPTER POINTS TO REMEMBER

1) When you are working to clear up a negative situation with people, take care to use no more power than is necessary.

2) If you find the first ritual not quite enough, then use the Ritual to Destroy Your Enemy's Power to Harm You, and if necessary after that Ritual to Drive Away Troublesome People. Between these three rituals, you can assure yourself of a life free from the negative influence of your previous enemies.

3) Never go to court or to major legal negotiations without first using the Ritual to Obtain Favor in Court. Your experience will prove the value of this ritual EVERY TIME.

4) You can revive a failing love affair with the Spell to Bind a Loved One to You.

5) All your important correspondence deserves the added power of the Ritual for Favorable Treatment of Your Letter. It will materially improve the acceptance of your proposals and ideas.

6) The Ritual for Acceptance By A New Group is a tremendous help whenever you find yourself heading into a new situation. Use it and enjoy complete acceptance.

7) The Complete Ritual for Building Personal Power can enrich and enhance your life beyond your most cherished hopes. It's never too late to enjoy a life of power and happiness, try it and you will use it often.

Chapter Twelve

Exorcism–How to Get Rid of Demons, Harmful Obsessing Entities, and Negative Thoughtforms

Our civilization's continual increase in problems of mental health is blamed on the increasing pressures of life in our modern society, but a large part of the trouble stems from our scientific ignorance of spirit obsession and possession. That the ancients understood obsession-possession and its treatment is clearly shown in a classic case given in the Bible, Mathew 9: 28-32:

> "And when he was come to the other side into the country of the Gargesenes, there met him two possessed with devils coming out of the tombs, exceeding fierce, so that no man might pass by that way. And behold, they cried out, saying, 'What have we to do with thee, Jesus, thou Son of God? Art thou come hither to torment us before time?' And there was a good way off from them an herd of many swine feeding. So the devils besought him, saying, 'If thou cast us out, suffer us to go away into the herd of swine.' And he said unto them, 'Go.' And when they were come out, they went into the herd of swine; and, behold, the whole herd of swine ran violently down a steep place into the sea and perished in the waters."

Epicurus among the Greeks was well known as an exorcist and King Solomon of the Jews was an admitted master of it. Within our modern experience, the Evangelist, Billy Graham, has written of his personal battles with "the Devil," including an instance where Billy Graham states that the Devil set his typewriter on fire. To deny the existence of negative spirit beings and live in ignorance is to court disaster. Our mental hospitals are full of people who could be returned to normal, productive lives with the proper service of exorcism.

Obsession and Possession in the Twentieth Century

A nearly hysterical voice on my telephone said: "Al, in my meditations I keep getting the word, *vampire*. There was an entity in my hall making wild noises last night, and I'm afraid that if it gets into my bedroom I'm a goner!" A little discussion convinced me that the lady really had an entity problem, so we went to work on it together. It took just about every technique we will give you in this chapter to win, but three days later the same lady called to report in a happy, relaxed voice that she is again free and able to go about her life without fear of harm from a negative spirit entity.

An Experience with "Possession"

What happens if you don't catch it in time? And find that the physical body of the normal person is controlled by an "outside" intelligence. My first personal experience with possession dates back to 1957. I had been asked to assist with spiritual healing for a man whom we will call L.D. He had undergone several operations for the steady deterioration of the vertebrae in his neck, but there was no relief from the pain. Two of us were performing the spiritual healing process—a lady was standing behind L.D. sending energy into his head and neck from her hands, while I sat about three feet in front of the patient adding energy from my hands to the two of them. Suddenly L.D.'s body stiffened into a full trance and a different voice began speaking through it. The spirit had been a fighter pilot in World War I and was momentarily reliving an air battle. Then we got the spirit's attention and engaged it in conversation. It told us it was L.D.'s deceased brother who had committed suicide several years before by hanging himself with the cord from an electric appliance. The spirit had never forgiven its brother for not arriving home in time to prevent the suicide, and it was punishing L.D. by attaching itself to the neck (symbolic of the spirit's broken neck from the hanging) and causing the pain and bone deterioration. It took a great deal of salesmanship and some help from the spirit world to convince the spirit that it had better things to do than continually torment its brother. But it was done, and the pain began to subside almost immediately.

It is also my opinion that the "murder" of Robert Kennedy was committed while the body of the man Sirhan was controlled by a violent spirit entity. And this gives us another good reason to guard against possession—the law holds *you* responsible for all the acts of of your physical body whether your consciousness is controlling it or someone else's. Psychiatric tests would not necessarily uncover possession because the entity could be smart enough to leave the victim completely alone during any examination.

Positive Forms of Spirit Possession in Our Modern World

Before we get into the depths of exorcism, let's take a moment to examine the positive aspects of spirit possession. The phenomenon called *trance* is a form of spirit possession that has been used positively for centuries to bring guidance and help to the "living" from the realms of what man erroneously calls the "dead." Probably the best known trance medium of modern times is the late Author Ford whose televised trance session brought the voice of a "dead" son to Bishop James A. Pike and thereby stirred up a great deal of fresh interest in life beyond the grave.

I am thoroughly convinced of the value of trance for spirit contact—I do quite a bit of it myself and it has been much more than mere inspiration for me. It has brought warnings of potential dangers to avoid, new business ventures, stock market tips, guidance in love affairs and all manner of good things to me personally and to those who have used the spirit advice that came through my tranced body. But we should consider entering the trance state with the same caution we would exercise in lending an uninsured automobile to another person—be sure you can trust the ability as well as integrity of the spirit person to whom you may lend your body. It is not our purpose to teach you trance in this chapter, but if space permits we will touch the "how to" in our closing chapter. Right now, we are seeking simply the firmer understanding of spirit/human relationships.

Automatic writing and the ouija board also involve degrees of spirit possession. Because these practices are often attempted by people who lack knowledge of psychic protection techniques, they have accumulated a reputation for being very dangerous. In fact, they are exactly as dangerous as meeting a stranger in a human body. If you recognize that the "other side" or "spirit world" contains people of widely varying capability and integrity (just as the physical world does), and act with caution in meeting spirit strangers, you should be quite safe. But it is still abvisable to be well versed in powerful exorcism techniques, "just in case."

How to Recognize Attempts at Obsession, or Possession of Your Body

Your well-developed *constructive will* is a natural defense against obsession and possession, thus anything that tends to weaken your will may be the beginning workings of a possession attempt. Nothing is quite so pathetic as a powerful obsession/possession problem because the victim's family and friends generally think of him (or her) as psychotic, "crazy," or at best some kind of a "ding-bat." Let's take a good look at the symptoms to be sure that something like this can't happen to *you*.

Chronic Pains that your doctor can't explain or eliminate are often the result of deliberate entity attack. We mentioned the problem of L.D. previously in this chapter where the spirit attacked his neck in "vengeance" for the spirit's suicide by hanging. Other favorite places for entity attack are the head, feet, joints, heart and stomach. One classic case was related to us after the patient had suffered a most difficult medical cure.

D.S. had become interested in automatic writing and allowed a spirit entity to use her arm for the purpose. The spirit at first convinced D.S. that it was her own "high self" and that she should follow all of its instructions. To insure obedience, the spirit promised to clamp a blinding headache on her whenever its will was not followed. When the instructions from the spirit began to be more and more ridiculous, a pitched battle for control of the organism ensued. D.S. went to the most enlightened source of medical help. The doctors called in handwriting experts who stated that the automatic writing exhibited the characteristics of an eleven-year-old girl (D.S. was in her late forties at the time) and it was markedly different from D.S.'s normal writing. The doctors instructed D.S. to defy the spirit and gave her some powerful pain pills to combat the resulting headaches. In time the spirit got tired of its game and went on to find a more willing dupe. Thus D.S. recovered, but she lost a potentially good tool because she was deathly afraid of any form of spirit contact from that day to this.

The first line of defense against this form of attack is to know your body well. Don't accept a diagnosis of "incurable" or "unknown" causes. When in doubt, use the exorcism techniques we will give you. There is no reason to live anything but a happy, healthy life free from pain and/or entity attack. Make it so for *you.*

Voices or Strong Compulsive Feelings

These are often used by unruly spirit entities to control a "human being." Sometimes it is just to confuse and torment the victim, but there are cases, as with Sirhan Sirhan, where the intent is malicious use of your body for murder, rape, or mayhem.

Jack Y. told us of a time in a hotel room when a voice suggested that he open the window. It seemed like a good idea, so he did. Then came the feeling of a compulsion to jump! And he was twelve stories up at the time! He knew enough to fight it, and used the exorcism techniques to free himself. Otherwise it would have been listed as "suicide."

Many women who live alone are bothered by obscene voices from the negative spirit realms. On the positive side, Joan of Arc's voices led her to great accomplishments, but the world wasn't ready, and we know what happened to her! They wouldn't burn you at the stake today, but it's still prudent to be extremely careful what kind of spirit voices you listen to—and even more important to use care where you admit it. When in doubt, *exorcise!* It won't hurt the highly-evolved spirits, but it surely gets rid of the lesser ones.

Lapses of Memory

Lapses can indicate that you were controlled by an outside agency for a short time. If this happens to you often, it's a good idea to use the exorcism techniques regularly—even if you think there is a good medical explanation for your problem. In time the medical profession will take more of the psychic/spirit world into account, but meanwhile there is no reason to let a materially-oriented medical man unwittingly help an entity make your life a disaster area. Common sense tells you to seek medical assistance whenever there is a physical problem. But a good exorcism ritual may help even more. And you don't care who gets credit for the healing as long as you are healthy and *free*.

Bloating of Your Body or Sudden Gains of Weight are often the result of entity interference with your natural metabolism, probably as a preliminary to attempting more direct control. As your self-image and constructive will are weakened by this process, you become more open to control by unscrupulous spirit entities. Take yourself in hand, diet-wise of course, but an exorcism ritual may prove even more beneficial.

Aberrations in Your Thinking Process

Aberrations strongly indicate outside spirit use of your organism. In my own trance work my best description of the preliminary stages is "letting the spirit think inside my head." Then because my spirit control, Prof. Reinhardt, is German and I am of Welsh-English descent, I tease, "But if I find myself lapsing into a German accent in some unguarded moment, the Prof. will have to go"! This is quite similar to our *rules for recognizing psychic attack* from Chapter 9. Examine all thoughts, urges and negative feelings to be sure they are not planted in you by an outside agency. And again, when in doubt, *Exorcise!*

Your Articles of Personal Jewelry, etc.
Appearing in Strange Places

Such happenings may be the work of friendly spirits trying to get your attention. But it could also be the early stages of a powerful plan of obsession/possession directed at you. Spirit entities can indeed move solid matter, and the unscrupulous may use this as a method of bringing you to doubt your own sanity and thus open you to more direct control.

We have suggested the more obvious symptoms of obsession and possession to give you a feel for the subject matter. Some control attempts are subtle indeed and may proceed for weeks or even months before the victim realizes the trouble he is in. The old adage, "Eternal vigilance is the price of freedom" certainly applies to matters of obsession and possession. But the basic protection rituals are not all that difficult—so we can repeat our theme of this section, *when in doubt, exorcise!*

Incense and a Short Ritual for Dispelling Negative Entities

The recipe for a good entity exorcising incense is:

1/4 tsp. Brimstone (Powdered)	1 tbsp. Vanillan Powder
1 tbsp. Orris Powder	1 tsp. Jalop Powder
2 tbsp. Rosemary (powdered)	1 pinch Saltpeter
2 tbsp. Powdered Charcoal	1 tbsp. All-Purpose Flour
1/4 dram Patchouli Oil	1/4 dram Jasmine Oil
1 oz. Tincture of Benzoin	

Powder the solid ingredients and mix well in your mortar and pestle. Mix the liquid ingredients and dissolve the saltpeter in them. Add the solid ingredients to the liquid ingredients and stir into a thick mud like mass. Spread the mixture in a tin or plastic box about 1/4 inch thick. When it is nearly dry, cut it into incense cubes.

The ritual is performed for nine consecutive nights for best results. Light blue altar candles, attune with the Blue Light, light your entity exorcising incense and chant:

> Unwanted creatures, hear my word.
> Away with you! Fly like a bird.
> Leave us now in my command,
> Within these walls you may not stand.
> Go in peace I order thee.
> And as my will, so mote it be!

How a Voice Obsession Was Healed

For three weeks Sarina B. had awakened at 3:00 a.m. each morning to the sound of voices abusing her in very obscene language. At first she was afraid to mention it to anybody for fear of being called crazy. Finally she got up the courage to talk with me about her frightening experience. The incense ritual was suggested. Sarina gathered her ingredients and made the incense that same evening. When she lit the incense, a stern voice commanded, "Put that smelly stuff out"! But she stood her ground and chanted with great determination. In response the entities cursed most vilely, but as Sarina kept chanting, the voices faded in power. She kept chanting for several minutes after the voices were gone. Nothing woke her up the next morning, so she had a wonderfully restful night's sleep for the first time in three weeks. Sarina continued the ritual for the next eight nights to be sure, and has never been bothered again. But she keeps a supply of the incense in a tin box near her altar, "just in case."

Possession/Obsession Breaking Sprinkling Solution

We normally use a sprinkling solution of salt in water for our protective ritual work, but when there are indications of the attempt at obsession or possession, stronger measures are needed. This sprinkling solution is made as follows:

4 oz. Water	4 oz. Vinegar
2 tbsp. Salt	1 tbsp. Basil (Powdered)
1 tbsp. Bay Laurel (Powdered)	1 tsp. Jalop Powder

Make two batches of the solution. Divide the first batch into two parts and put it in small glasses, one at the front door and one at the back. Take the the second batch to your altar and use it at the end of the basic protection ritual. Sprinkle your altar area, and if you feel the need, your whole house, with the solution as you chant:

> Mighty power of this brew,
>   Exorcise all spirits who
> Would haunt, obsess, or me possess.
>   Send them to a place of rest.
> Banish all who would control,
>   Take them to the place of old
> Where they must learn to see the Light,
>   And evermore to do what's right.
> Haunting ones from here must go,
>   Or be ye burned! I say it's so!
> Harken to this word from me,
>   And as my will, so mote it be!

A Case of Practical Benefits Through Exorcism

The symptoms were strange, ugly odors around the house that could not be accounted for, opening and shutting of cupboard doors in the middle of the night, strangely misplaced articles around the house and a sound like heavy breathing in the bedroom. It was enough to convince E.C. that some form of exorcism was necessary before things got worse. As he chanted and sprinkled the solution in bedrooms and kitchen, he heard strange cries and wails. But be continued his ritual undaunted. It took three consecutive nights to complete the task, but finally all the manifestations were eliminated—and as E.C. commented, "Even the plants around the house perked up and seemed healthier. And you may call it coincidence, but a long awaited promotion on my job came within three days after the exorcism was completed."

Preventative Techniques—How to Avoid the Preliminary Attempts at Obsession or Possession

The protective work of Chapter 9 applies here with even more importance. Any form of psychic attack or the evil eye against you tends to open you up to the negative beings who would seek to obsess and possess you. Thus using the Posssession/Obsession Breaking Sprinkling Solution in combination with the Ritual for Protection of Your Home should enhance the power of each. And the sachet bag above your door can be reenforced with a string of fresh garlic. The garlic and the glasses of sprinkling solution should be renewed or replaced once a week, preferably on Saturday.

It is especially important in this work to remember that an effective Witch is an eclectic. Borrow the powerful parts of any and all religions, occult practices, medicine—use your consecrated jewelry, the Saturn Pentacle, your Ankh and anything else that may remotely add to your power. And keep yourself *calm.* The negative entities literally feed on the energy of your fear and frustration, so a good way to discourage them is to starve them to death. The brightness of your aura that gleams with the power of *constructive will* serves you well as a protector. Let nothing weaken your constructive will—accept no discouragement, frustration, or feeling of failure or defeat! As your evolving power brings success and victory in other areas, your confidence in your ability to use what you have learned brings more power—and soon *nothing of the darkness will dare come near you.*

Complete Exorcism Ritual for Removal of Entities and Negative Forces

If the short rituals and protective devices given here and in Chapter 9 have not completely eliminated the negative influences around you and your home, the complete exorcism ritual is necessary. Plan this ritual to begin at 7:00 p.m. on the Saturday after a full moon. The evening before you start the complete ritual, use the Possession/Obsession Breaking/Sprinkling Solution in its ritual and sprinkle it throughout the house, taking care to get some in all corners of every room and closet. In preparation for the full ritual, lay out your nine and seven foot circles and put your altar in the center. (See Chapter 9.) Gather everything you will need for the ritual inside the circles before you begin.

In addition to your normal altar supplies, you will need (1) white candles for your altar candleholders (2) one or two cubes of incense for Dispelling Negative Entities (3) a small quantity of powdered Brimstone (4) exorcism oil—I suggest equal parts of patchouli, sandalwood and jasmine (5) your chalice or a glass of Possession/Obsession Breaking Sprinkling Solution (6) an ankh or Saturn Pentacle that you will wear for protection constantly after the ceremony (7) Your Witch's cord and Athamé.

With all the materials assembled, and your altar set so that you face *east* as you sit at it, you are ready to begin.

Ritual Step #1: Sit down at your altar and begin building an ever growing sphere of White Light with you at its center, as you chant:

> Rama, Agni, send the Light to me.
> > Rama, Agni, send the powerful Light to me.
> Sweep away the things that harm,
> > Let them cause me no alarm.
> Rama, Agni, send the Light that sets me free.

Ritual Step #2: Pick up your Athamé and salute the *east*. Walk to the *east* edge of your nine foot circle and ritually draw it with the point of your Athamé, proceeding counter-clockwise through north, west, south and back to east as you use the Shiva chant:

> Lovely, powerful Shiva, God of sweeping change,
> > Sweep away the lesser, shut it out of range.
> Leave the beauty and the Light, bright and clean and fair.
> > Remove all vibrations of misery and despair.
> Leave this place and these fine things, fresh and bright and pure,
> > Holy as your own fine self, bright, complete and sure.
> Lovely, powerful Shiva, my thanks to you I give,
> > That from your sweeping power in beauty may I live.

Ritual Step #3: Return to your altar, replace your Athame, and light your altar candles. Chant:

> Creatures of fire, this charge I give:
> No evil in my presence live,
> No phantom, spook, nor spell may stay
> Around this place, not night nor day.
> Hear my word addressed to thee,
> And as my will, so mote it be!

Ritual Step #4: Pick up your chalice of Possession/Obsession Breaking Sprinkling Solution and proceed to the inner edge of your nine foot circle. Carefully sprinkle the solution inside the circle, proceeding in a counter-clockwise direction as you chant:

> Might power of this brew,
> Exorcise all spirits who
> Would haunt, obsess, or me possess.
> Send them to a place of rest.
> Banish all who would control,
> Take them to the place of old
> Where they must learn to see the Light,
> And evermore to do what's right.
> Haunting ones from here must go,
> Or be ye burned! I say it's so!
> Harken to this word from me,
> And as my will, so mote it be!

Ritual Step #5: Return to your altar, replace the chalice and pick up your Athame. Again salute the east and proceed to the east edge of your seven foot circle. Ritually draw the seven foot circle with your Athame as you repeat the Shiva chant. Again proceed in a counter-clockwise direction.

Ritual Step #6: Return to your altar, replace the Athame and pick up your chalice of Possession/Obsession Breaking Sprinkling Solution. Go to the east edge of the seven foot circle and sprinkle the inside of the circle as you chant: Mighty power of this brew. . . .

Ritual Step #7: Return to your altar and replace the chalice. Light a piece of the incense for Dispelling Negative Entities. Place it in your incense burner and chant:

Unwanted creatures, hear my word.
Away with you! Fly like a bird.
Leave us now is my command,
Within these walls you may not stand.
Go in peace, I order thee,
And as my will, so mote it be!

Ritual Step #8: Anoint all of your body's orifices, your brow, throat, heart, solar plexus and genital area with the exorcism oil and chant:

And now this oily essence fair
Adds its great power to the air,
Attracting spirits of the Light,
Protecting me both day and night,
This charge is true and proper, see.
And as my will, so mote it be!

Ritual Step #9: Anoint your ankh or Saturn Pentacle with exorcism oil and chant: (Here I am using the ankh consecration chant. If you are using the pentacle substitute its chant.)

Ankh of power, full of life,
Protect me evermore from strife.
Bound to me by word and Light,
Keep me safe both day and night.
A strong protector unto me,
And as my will, so mote it be!

Ritual Step #10: Put on your ankh or pentacle (and don't remove it until you are certain that all attacking influences are banished permanently). Light a second piece of the Incense for Dispelling Negative Entities and add it to the burning incense in your burner. Lightly sprinkle the burning incense with a pinch of brimstone and chant:

And now, great spirits of the Light,
This is where we win my fight!
Obsessing ones who still are near
Must be shown what they do fear.
See that each one knows full well,
This brimstone is a taste of hell.

The place where bound they each will be
   If e'er again they come near me.
A life of power now I lead,
   My true command each one must heed.
Triumphant now, as all must see,
   And as my will, so mote it be!

Ritual Step #11: Close the ritual with thanks to all: "Great Spirits of Light who have helped me here, my heartfelt thanks for this and your continuing help and guidance. To all elementals gathered here, go in peace now to your appointed tasks, and when you are finished return to your natural places, harming no one on the way. My thanks to all. Blessed be"!

How a Strange Haunting Was Stopped

I.J. had suffered for almost three years—each morning she woke up to find new scratch marks on her face and arms. She had been unable to keep a job for more than a month, and the obsessing voices constantly taunted her: "You must become a prostitute, that is the only way we will let you make a living." She had no friends, and her family was convinced she should be committed to an institution. With all her remaining strength, I.J. began the complete ritual we have just given you. She repeated it for three consecutive nights, then on the morning of the fourth day she received a call from an old acquaintance. He told I.J. that last evening the lover I.J. had spurned three years ago had a sudden stroke and died on the way to the hospital. "Coincidentally" all the obsessing entities were gone and I.J. quickly returned to her normal, clear skinned, happy self. She landed a good job and is happily a solid member of the community once more.

CHAPTER POINTS TO REMEMBER

1) Our mental hospitals are full of obsession and possession cases. Healings may be possible through exorcism of obsessions.

2) Obsession and possession are as real in the Twentieth Century as they were in the time of King Solomon, Epicurus and the early Christian era.

3) There are positive forms of possession such as mediumistic

trance or automatic writing. But great care is necessary before surrendering your body. Be certain you can rely on the ability as well as integrity of the spirit.

4) Symptoms of attempts at negative possession or obsession are: chronic pains, voices or strong compulsive feelings, lapses of memory, bloating of your body or sudden gains of weight, aberrations in your thinking processes, articles of your jewelry or other possessions appearing in incongruous places, any apparent attempt to weaken your constructive will or fill you with discouragement.

5) The Incense for Dispelling Negative Entities and its short ritual will generally break up an entity attack—if you start soon enough.

6) The Possession/Obsession Breaking Sprinkling Solution and its chant used throughout the house is good for ridding you or a place of negative entities.

7) If rituals five and six haven't done the whole job of exorcism, use the Complete Exorcism Ritual for Removal of Entities and Negative Forces.

Chapter Thirteen

How to Enhance
Your Witchcraft Powers
with Sex Magic

*T*he origins of Witchcraft go way back in time and stem from mankind's need to be in tune with natures's forces to insure good crops, good hunting, and plenty of children—all to insure the perpetuation of the species. In the ancient days, the number one god was the great horned one, Cernunnos, who was (and to many still is) a fertility god. The very horns of Cernunnos are phallic symbols, showing the ancients' understanding of the magical as well as reproductive power of the sex energy. Powerful phallic symbology (figures of the male genital organ) is found in the early Hindu religions, and indeed in all of the so–called primitive religions. Then as man grew to rely more on his technology and machines, the understanding of the magic of phallic power was lost to all but a few. Let's examine it for the purpose of harnessing it to amplify the power of your ritual work.

The Nature and Magical Power of the Reproductive Force

Many of the ancient grimoires (Witchcraft proceedings) contain passages regarding preparation for a specific ritual that instruct the practitioner to "abstain from sexual congress for seven days prior to performing this ritual." Some even require abstention for thirty days! The idea is to dam up this most powerful of nature's energies and let it explode into the ritual as an irresistible force. Similarly the Kundalini Yoga techniques are designed to lift the magic power of the procreative force to the head and so usher the Yogi into Samadhi or true spiritual enlightenment. But unreasonable sex repression is dangerous at best, as we were clearly shown by the writings of Sigmund Freud, the famous psychoanalyst.

To get a better understanding of the psychic/magic side of the reproductive drive, consider the energy and intelligence demonstrated by the salmon which fight their way from the ocean up rivers and streams to the place of their own hatching. Such singleness of purpose is seldom seen in men, and for that dauntless salmon the purpose is clear, *reproduction*, or in human terms, *sex*. That there are great extra-sensory powers involved in animal sex is demonstrated much closer to home. Next time your (or your neighbor's) female dog comes into heat, try cataloging the number of male dogs hanging around, and the distance each has traveled to get there. When you stop to think about it, you realize that the navigational skills of migratory birds, seals and fish are also directly related to this mystic power of nature expressed as the reproductive drive. If there is such a thing as the irresistible force in nature, we must conclude that it is the expression of the sex or reproductive drive. Obviously this power has tremendous positive potentials for the budding Witch (you) who learns to harness it for practical use.

The Trick of Using Abstinence to Power a Spell

The world's great religions obviously respect the power of the sex drive, but it has been woefully mistreated by some of the "teachers" due to simple misunderstanding. Parts of the Hindu and Christian teachings have been misconstrued to mean that the sex act should be performed only for the purpose of adding new members to the species. This is as intelligent as saying that water must be used for drinking purposes only, not for generating steam or hydro-electric power. Thus the normal practice of abstinence from sex activity or celibacy is virtually worthless for generating the spiritual and psychic energy of accomplishment. *Without the "TRICK," celibacy is a complete waste of vital energy!*

Here is the trick! The traditional methods of practicing celibacy include careful concentration on other things to avoid sexual arousal. The idea is to dampen or bank the fires of passion until they eventually die out, thus supposedly leaving the energy available for the higher spiritual pursuits. But the net effect of such practice is a lessening of the total power available for use by the individual. The trick is in thinking and acting in a sexually provocative manner, but using your constructive will to keep the great power in check until it is brought to bear in truly explosive but constructive fashion in a magical ceremony of Witchcraft.

How to Use the Trick of Abstinence to Make Your Spells Unbeatable

If you are married or "living with" someone, you should explain what you are doing and enlist your partner's willing cooperation, and we will assume their cooperative participation, in your ritual work. But if you live alone or with a highly uncooperative partner, you will need to be more innovative and imaginative. In either case, plan for your really important ritual a full week in advance.

Consider the week as the exciting foreplay to your most fantastic "conquest." Start mildly, but as the week goes by build your desire energy up to the explosion point. The requirement is to spend some time each day at the build-up, and the more the better—flirt, pet, tease, read racy magazines and stories, go to "X-rated" movies, do anything that really "turns you on." Come as close as you like as often as possible, but you must exercise your constructive will to abstain from the sex act itself. The constructive will is charged to say,"I will keep building up this energy for the witchcraft ritual, there will be no release until the ritual is performed."

By the time the ritual itself begins, you should be so "fired-up" you are nearly "out of your head." Then pour yourself in the *thoughtform* building previously described and let all that pent-up sex energy flow into your new creation! It is misunderstanding of the method and power of this practice that has led to some of the strange cult work and at times bad publicity for the beautiful use of the sex drive (nature's greatest force) to make a ritual really go. This practice will add power to any of your rituals, but it should be used sparingly—after all the human organism was not designed to run at full throttle all the time. Rest and normal healthy sexual activity are also necessary to balance. But when you are having trouble with a really important problem, this is the source of the extra power that can lead to total victory.

How Harry and Charlene Used Sex Magic to Get Out of Financial Trouble

Harry and Charlene S. were deep in debt. While Harry was in the hospital recovering from a kidney operation, the company where he was a journeymen machinist had been closed by its new owners. Harry experienced difficulty finding a new job, with only temporary, low-paying work available.

Meanwhile, their daughter, Martha, developed acute apendicitis and her operation was not covered by insurance. While Martha was in the hospital, Charlene became interested in Witchcraft with our group and influenced Harry into working with her in Witchcraft. Their health and prosperity rituals seemed to stop the piling up of new debt, but they were uncomfortably far behind in too many payments. So they decided to add the power of the excited sex drive to a new prosperity ritual.

The preparation was a week of happy torture. Harry came home from work to candle light dinners with Charlene who made herself a fantastic temptress—and every evening was spent in trying out new and exciting methods of seduction. There were several moments when constructive will almost went out the window in favor of a wildly climactic love scene, but they managed to persevere and go to their witchcraft altar at the end of the week highly motivated for the sex magic ritual as set out at the end of this chapter.

They used the Complete Money/Prosperity Drawing Ritual and poured a week of pent-up passion into a beautiful *thoughtform* of rainbows and waves, rivers and streams, buckets and wheelbarrows of *money*. Though they felt that they were still novices at Witchcraft, they certainly felt that this had been a most powerful ritual for their benefit.

Harry landed a good job at more money than he had ever made before just three days later, and the end of a week brought a surprise check in the mail for just over $10,000! The check was from the estate of a distant uncle from whom they had expected nothing! Suddenly all their debts were paid and there was a nice nest egg for next year's vacation which they suddenly planned as a second honeymoon.

Positive Use of the Sex Energy
for Spell and Thoughtform Creation

The tremendous power of the sex drive energy is available to all who accept it as "God-given" and pure. If you have lingering feelings of impropriety or guilt about the preceding section, it is important to work for a better understanding of yourself before embarking on the more powerful uses of the sex drive. You must accept the human body and the sex act as wholesome and pure. The only thing remotely evil about it is the twisted impressions that occasionally get loose in people's minds. Root out any negative ideas you may have about this natural drive and accept it as a precious gift from your Creator.

The ideal union involves the simultaneous joining of at least the four basic aspects of your natures (spirit, mind, emotion and physical body) in the mutual givingness of pure love. The result of such an ideal sexual union is a new dimension of pure power—as well as a new dimension of spiritual sexual experience that is as indescribable as the mystic experience itself. It involves a truly perfect union, brought about by dissolving all barriers that may have existed between the partners or between either individual and the fullness of the sex act. The preparations logically include mutual exploration of the breadth and depth of each other's beingness. It grows only in an atmosphere that is completely free of taboos, "no-no's," criticism, or the withholding of anything. Any mental or psychological artificial "holding back" will inhibit the flow of the very creative power you seek to tap.

The power is generated by use of the sexual union for the purpose of energy transfer. It is essential that enough constructive will be established that premature ejaculation by the male partner is not a danger. Many of the occult and ancient witchcraft documents teach use of the sexual congress for the purpose of energy transfer only, and orgasm itself is treated as a major breech of etiquette. This is an excellent method for transference of healing energies to the mutual benefit of both of the partners, and practice in energy transference is a reasonable prelude to the more powerful use of the energy. A good union for this purpose should last from one to three hours, including maximum excitation of both partners, but using the constructive will of each to avoid the orgasm itself.

How Janet C. Experienced a Healing of the Liver

Janet C. returned home from the doctor's office in a state of near panic. The X-rays had indicated a tumor on her liver. A second examination was scheduled in two weeks with the idea of setting the date for the operation. In her discussion with John her husband, the idea of attempting healing through energy transference was discussed. They decided to try sessions as outlined in this chapter equally spaced before the next examination. There was a special sort of "glow" to the sharing of the energy which both parties spent much mental effort in directing to Janet's liver. After each session there was a feeling of great accomplishment, and the one the night before the examination felt especially powerful. There was a note of astonishment in the doctor's voice when the second set of X-rays revealed no sign of a tumor. Janet was pronounced in excellent health and she has remained so for several years.

How to Use the Sex Energy
for Powerful Thoughtform and Spell Creation

Once the art of energy transference is well-mastered, you are ready to learn the ultimate use of the sexual energy in *thoughtform* creation. The partners must of course agree in advance on the purpose for which the generation of this energy is to be applied. This can be a broad purpose (such as prosperity, health or love) or a specific one (such as the sale of a piece of property, purchase of a new car, or a new job for one of the partners). Next the choosing of a simple symbol to represent your planned *thoughtform* is necessary. This should be simple enough to be drawn with just two or three pen strokes, for example you might represent prosperity as a dollar sign ($), or health with the letter "H."

For this work there must be plenty of time and a place provided where both partners feel completely safe and comfortable. The ideal here is the elimination of all psychological pressure or conflict so the fullness of each being can participate in generating the maximum energy flow. Naturally clothing of any sort is superfluous, and the room should be warm enough so that covers can be turned down and the bodies are comfortable while completely exposed to the air. The lighting may be bright or subdued according to the personal taste of the partners, but there should be at least enough candle light to allow the participation of your sense of vision in this beautiful ritual. The warm up or "love play" period should be completely spontaneous—again the key is the absence of psychological pressures or inhibitions. This is a time to develop the spontaneous cooperation between partners that breaks down any remaining psychological taboos. Set out to mutually enjoy the *entirety* of each other and invite your whole being to participate in this ritual.

Stress should be on the relaxation that allows maximum concentration on energy transference and the building of the *thoughtform*. During this beautiful period, the partners strive for a happy balance between excitation of the energy and the quiet periods of shaping it into the planned *thoughtform* that they want to accomplish. The normal duration of the congress will vary while the energy potential and union of their higher natures in the *thoughtform* production is brought to a peak. When a full unity of purpose of spirit, mind, emotion and body is realized, the partners join in a mutual climax that brings the *thoughtform* into unquestioned vital dynamic existence.

How a Sex Magic Thoughtform Saved a Business

Sally and Joe R. owned a family grocery store. When the pressure of competition from the large supermarkets began to seriously reduce their business, they adopted the basic prosperity techniques of Witchcraft. But even with this extra help they were barely squeeking by from month to month. Finally they decided to use the sex energy to power their prosperity *thoughtform* to the highest degree. Let's share the report as Sally sent it: "Our sex energy powered prosperity *thoughtform* is working wonders in the store! It's almost unbelievable, but business is up better than thirty percent and new customers seem to be drawn to our store in a very magical way. The extra money comes in handy to say the least, but the expansion of the love element of our marriage would be worth the effort even if it hadn't worked the money miracle. We plan to rebuild the *thoughtform* at least once a month."

Complete Ritual for Harnessing the Sex Energy in a Powerful Thoughtform

We will give this ritual as it would be used for a prosperity *thoughtform*. The changes and adaptations to other uses will be obvious and should be made to suit your individual tastes.

Preparation for the ritual should include at least three days and up to seven days of provocative abstinence—each partner should go to great lengths to excite and arouse the other during this period to build the energy up to a peak. For the ritual itself, your altar should be set up in the bedroom. The head of the bed should face the north with the altar on the east side of the bed, facing east. Supplies in addition to your normal altar equipment should be gathered in advance as usual: (1) prosperity oil (2) prosperity incense (3) green-tapered candles for your altar candle holders (4) money drawing wash (See Chapter 7, p. 92) (5) money drawing powder (See recipe in Chapter 3, p. 50) (6) fresh rose petals (two nice size roses will give you enough petals). Take all necessary precautions to be sure you will not be interrupted, and go to your altar together with a complete absence of clothing or necklace type jewelry: Rings may be worn to add power to your ritual energy, but nothing more.

Ritual Step #1: Smile at the faces in your altar mirror and greet the nature spirits of your altar with a friendly greeting. Sit quietly and build the sphere of protective white Light around both of you. When you have visualized it clearly, invite the Light to turn a rich green color and chant together:

> Rama, Agni, send the Light to we.
>> Rami, Agni, send the lush green Light to we.
> Bathe us with your growth and love,
>> Send abundance from above.
> Rama, Agni, send the Light that sets us free.

Ritual Step #2: Light your altar candles and prosperity incense, and chant together:

> Oh, great and mighty Jupiter,
>> Your friendship we do seek.
> Your emissaries send to us,
>> Spirits rich and sleek.
> Good nature spirits sent by Jove,
>> Your comradeship we love.
> For bounty and good fellowship,
>> Our thanks are sent above.
> Spirits great, your riches share
>> In fun and friendship true.
> Prosperity descends on us,
>> Our thanks to lovely you.

> And now our Light is shining bright,
>> Rich green for all to see.
> Good fortune is our law of life.
>> With thanks, so mote it be!

Ritual Step #3: Lightly sprinkle the money drawing powder in a circle around the bed and around your altar. Then each partner anoints the other's brow, throat, heart, and solar plexus with the prosperity oil. Chant together:

> Our words have power as of old,
>> So hear us now, good Gnomes and Trolls.
> Bring us silver, bring us gold,
>> Bring the lush green stuff that folds.
> Come quickly now, have fun with us,
>> And treasure bring, you know you must.
> We speak to you with joy and glee,
>> And as our will, so mote it be!

Ritual Step #4: Joyfully sprinkle the bed itself with the rose petals, letting them fall in patterns of natural beauty all over the bed. Lightly sprinkle the altar area and a circle around the bed with the money drawing wash as you chant together:

> Nature spirits, hark to we,
>> Bring us opportunity.
> Bring us windfalls as good fun,
>> Winning horses one by one,
> Rising stocks, good poker hands,
>> Gifts of diamonds, platinum bands.
> Bring all gladly now to we,
>> And as our will, so mote it be!

Ritual Step #5: Find a comfortable position and lay quite still as you visualize the *thoughtform* energy gathering just above you. Mentally mould the energy into a tall, wide, funnel shaped channel. See the channel filling with money for you both as you speak aloud together:

The channel for our prosperity is built and is now being filled with rainbows and waves, rivers and streams, buckets and wheelbarrows full of money. It flows down upon us in an ever increasing flow of riches and abundance. We offer our grateful thanks to all the *thoughtforms* and spirits who are helping.

Bask in the joy and *reality* of the *thoughtform* and its resulting prosperity. Dream about its beauty and wonder aloud together. Alternate between the *thoughtform* building and feeding and the happy excitation of love.

Ritual Step #6: When you are both ready, join in a mutual climax of exploding light and lush green colors. Then affirm aloud together, *"It is born, now!"* And visualize aloud together the "rainbows and waves, rivers and streams . . . ." Then each party finger traces the dollar sign ($) on their body.

Ritual Step #7: Return to your altar together to close the ritual. Use the snuffer to extinguish the candles, then dismiss the elementals with thanks: "Our thanks to all the spirits and elementals who have participated here. To the elementals, you are dismissed. Go now to perform your appointed tasks, and when you are finished, return to your natural homes, harming no one on the way. Peace, love and thanks to all. Blessed be."

How Lois and Jim Reclaimed Their Prosperity

The results from this ritual are as good as you dare expect them to be. Lois and Jim Y. had become accustomed to a comfortable life from the good living Jim made selling real estate. Then during the late '60's and early '70's, the real estate market experienced a serious slowdown. Things finally got so bad for Lois and Jim that the bank was at the point of foreclosing the mortgage on their house, Lois got a part-time job to help out, but it seemed like a tiny drop in a very big bucket, so she looked for our witchcraft help for Jim. Here is her report: "Ecstasy! I finally got Jim to join me in the ritual for harnessing the sex energy into a powerful prosperity *thoughtform.* The results were better than I had dared hope. For the past eighteen months, Jim had been lucky to close one deal every three or four weeks. The first week after our ritual, he closed four! And the total is twelve for the month! The bank has quit bugging us, and things are heading for greater prosperity than we ever had before."

How C.K. Was Able to Sell His Business
at the Right Time for over $1 Million

C.K. had built a metal working business from a tiny hole in the wall to an almost two million dollar a year operation. It took twelve years of hard work and sacrifice. There were many setbacks because of the extremely cyclical nature of the business. Near the end of the accounting year that was twice the volume of the one before and highly profitable, C.K. realized that the next three years would be a big threat to the company's survival—all the major programs that had carried him this far were scheduled to phase out by the middle of next year. He had been thinking of selling the company for years, and this was the "now or never" opportunity.

He talked it over with his wife, Charlotte, and they decided to use the Complete Ritual For Harnessing The Sex Energy In A Powerful *Thoughtform* to sell the business while the time was right. He talked to his banker and a management consultant the morning before his ritual was scheduled to be performed, suggesting that his company was for sale.

That evening C.K. and Charlotte put a week of pent-up drive into a super-powerful *thoughtform.*

Less than a week later, the contact was made with a New York Stock Exchange Listed firm. The merger turned C.K.'s shaky $125,000 net worth into over a million dollars *after taxes!* And he stayed on as a prestige manager for the new company.

CHAPTER POINTS TO REMEMBER

1) Witchcraft originated from mankind's need to work with the forces of nature to produce good crops, good hunting, and many children. The ancient fertility rites stirred up a very powerful energy which is available to *you* today.

2) There is a magic and irresistibility to nature's most powerful drive as exhibited by the salmon's drive to return to its birthplace to spawn, and the tremendous navigational feats of migratory birds, seals and fish. You can harness this great power to work for your benefit.

3) Abstinence can be used to build up your energy potential for *thoughtform* building and ritual purposes. The trick to building up the power is to seek the excitement and arousal, but allow it no release except into your ritual *thoughtform* building work.

4) The practice of sexual energy transference can be used as a powerful instrument of healing or to add great power to your *thoughtforms.*

5) The ultimate use of the sexual energy is the powering of a

thoughtform that is built during the energy transfer stage and super-powered in mutual climax.

6) The Complete Ritual for Harnessing the Sex Energy in a Powerful *Thoughtform* is designed to bring together all of the powers of your Witchcraft into one irresistible force that must obey your well defined command.

Chapter Fourteen

How to Use Rituals and Spells to Induce Astral Travel and Prophetic Dreams

*T*he brash young salesman had asked the cute switchboard operator for a date several times, but always there was a polite refusal. To get her interested, Charlie decided to try an off-beat approach. Next evening he projected the odor of his pipe tobacco to her bedroom, while he did just a bit of "snooping." As he passed the switchboard in the morning, he casually commented, "That is a lovely orange nightgown you were wearing last night. Did you notice the aroma of my pipe?" When she sputtered in surprise, he didn't press the point, but headed smilingly to his own office. Next morning he just dropped a quick one as he passed the switchboard, "The lavendar one you wore last night is pretty, too." On the third morning, when Charlie was right again, it was more than human nature could stand. She demanded, "Just what are you doing to me anyway?" His quick answer was, "I'd be happy to explain it over dinner. Shall I pick you up about 7:30?" With an intrigued smile, she said, "Yes," and a happy love affair was launched. A somewhat frivolous, but practical application of astral projection.

The Practical Reality of the Astral

Throughout the whole of the occult/witchcraft lore, it is an accepted fact that the conscious, thinking part of a human being can be voluntarily projected for great distances outside the physical body. It is not our purpose to discuss the theory of this phenomenon here, we will confine ourselves to its practical methodology and application. If you would like more detail and alternate methods of projection, I suggest the 11th chapter of my book *Helping Yourself with Psycho-Cosmic Power.* * For the purpose of this practical witchcraft work let's agree that the vehicle which transports your consciousness outside the physical body is most often called the astral body. Other names for the astral vehicle are *emotional body* and *body of light*. There are degrees of consciousness and control of the out-of-the-body experience that have led people to call it by several names, the most common of which are *astral projection, soul flight,* and *bilocation.*

Practical Uses of Astral Projection

Before we turn to the "how to" of astral projection, let's examine the practical uses of this powerful phenomenon. The parapsychology department of U.C.L.A. has conducted experiments whereby a reasonably long number was written on a piece of paper and placed on top of a tall filing cabinet. The subject was placed on a couch near the floor and kept under constant observation. The challenge was to rise in the astral body, view the number on top of the file cabinet, return to the body and give the correct number. We will skip the safeguards against simple clairvoyance or telepathy and simple state that some subjects were successful. But this would be child's play to a well-trained Witch using procedures in this book.

Would you enjoy calling your sister in a distant city and complimenting her on her new couch the same day it is delivered? Want to know where your boyfriend goes when he is not with you? How about tracking down a runaway spouse, or reading your competitor's bid on a job before you deliver yours? And are you *sure* it is not being done to *you* already without your knowing about it?

Of greater importance to the serious student is the opportunity to visit loved ones and/or teachers who have passed beyond the veil called death. An "in person" visit to a financial wizard, a great scientist, or your own "spirit teacher" is much more useful and rewarding than the slower methods of contemplating a problem and hoping that guidance will come from your meditations!

*Parker Publishing Company, West Nyack, N.Y.

Preparation for Your Own Astral Travel

In the broad sense there are only two possible methods of achieving astral projection, either to separate the bodies while you are fully conscious, or to program your subconscious to wake you up after the bodies have naturally separated in the process called sleep. It is well known in the occult literature of Vedanta, Zoroastrianism, Huna and Theosophy that the natural process of sleep involves some separation of the astral body from its physical counterpart. Since there is a stress of anxiety for the beginning student who tries conscious separation, it is easier for most to gain a degree of familiarity with astral travel by first using one or more of the "wake up" techniques. What can you expect? And how shall you know that you are on the astral?

When you leave your body in a fully conscious state, gaze down at the apparently sleeping physical form, and calmly walk away, you will have a pretty good idea that you have completed an astral trip. But even then, the conscious mind may try to convince you that you were only "dreaming." So how can you tell that you were "out" when you started from the sleep state? The evidence is in the *color.* When seen from the astral vantage point, even the drabbest of rooms takes on a special brightness. There are no words to describe the vividness and beauty of the astral colors, but once you have seen them, you will understand and know that you have succeeded in visiting this fascinating and useful realm of life.

How Jewelry Was Found Through the Astral Ritual

Shirley W. had misplaced a very valuable ring and began to fear that it was lost forever. As a last resort, she decided to try looking from the astral as taught in our classes. Shirley used the subconscious mind programming ritual we will give you next. This is her report: "I used the ritual at bed time last night. About 3:00 a.m. this morning, I woke up with a vivid memory of seeing the fantastic colors which you have described to me as evidence that I was seeing on the astral. The scene was the small chest where I keep my fancy silverware. There, nestled under a big spoon was a shiny object that I took to be my ring. I got out of bed and went to look. Sure enough, there was the ring right where I saw it on the astral! I don't yet understand how it got there, but I'm happy to have it back and also happy to know that I enjoyed my first astral trip."

Ritual to Program Your Subconscious Mind to Induce Astral Travel

This ritual is best performed at bed time, but it can be used just before you lay the body down to take a short nap any time of the day or night. You will need an astral travel inducing oil and incense. The oil is a mixture of equal parts of citrus, frankessence, and myrrh. The astral travel incense recipe is:

1/2 oz. Sandalwood Powder	1/2 oz. Lavendar (powdered)
1/4 oz. Bayberry (powdered)	1/4 oz. Orris Root (powdered)
1/4 oz. Rose Petals (powdered)	1 oz. Powdered Charcoal
1 dram Frankessence (oil)	1/2 dram Patchouli (oil)
1-1/2 oz. Tincture of Benzoin	1/16 oz. Saltpeter

Mix your liquid ingredients and dissolve the saltpeter in them. Powder your herbs and mix the solid ingredients in your mortar and pestle, then gradually add them to the liquid. Smooth the mud like mass into a small tin, let it dry for 1/2 hour, then cut it into incense cubes as usual.

It is best to use this ritual during the period that begins two days after a new moon and ends two days before the full moon. Avoid astral travel on the nights of the new moon or a full moon until you are well experienced and know that you can handle yourself well. The astral travel oil and incense, and white candles will suffice for the ritual along with your normal altar supplies. Take extra precautions to be sure that your body will not be disturbed while you are out of it, and I assume that your altar is set up near a bed or couch.

Ritual Step #1: Sit at your altar and build a sphere of bright white Light in your visualization. You are at the center as usual. Chant:

> Rama, Agni, send the Light to me.
>   Rama, Agni, send the astral Light to me.
> Let it teach me how to fly,
>   That my soul may soar on high.
> Rama, Agni, send the Light that sets me free.

Ritual Step #2: Light your candles and astral travel incense, and chant:

> Creatures of fire, this charge to thee,
>> My astral body now set free
> To visit teachers of the Light,
>> Commune with loved ones this fine night.
> To live and learn and dance, you see,
>> In peace and perfect harmony.
> My body safe, do keep for me,
>> And as my will, so mote it be!

Ritual Step #3: Anoint your brow with the astral travel oil, and chant:

> Wondrous spirits of the air,
>> This lovely fragrance let us share.
> This oil upon my brow reminds
>> My very own subconscious mind
> To wake me on the astral plane
>> And know that both of us will gain
> As Light and Love we share with friends,
>> And knowledge gain that knows no ends.
> This is my word addressed to thee,
>> And as my will, so mote it be!

Ritual Step #4: Conclude the sitting up part of the ritual: "And now my thanks to all spirits who have helped me here. I invite the spirit teachers and loved ones to meet me as I awaken on the astral plane that I may share your company. To all elementals assembled here, attend me now as I prepare to leave my body, and when we are finished, return to your natural homes, harming no one on the way. I come now into the pleasure of your presence. Blessed be." (It is optional, but I suggest that you extinguish your altar candles at this point.)

Ritual Step #5: Lay your body down comfortably on the bed or couch, close your eyes and allow yourself to drift off into a comfortable sleep, knowing that you will remember your astral experience when you return to your body and "wake it up."

How to Be Accurately Aware of Your Astral Travels

It is important to digest your experiences in peace and confidence when you bring the memories back to your normal waking state in the physical body. There is a temptation to jump to erroneous conclusions, particularly after the first two or three "trips." Here is M.C.'s experience that shows what can happen: "I became conscious that I was on the astral, apparently traveling in a silent aircraft. We were gliding close to the ground and I could see details of the under brush and a large fallen log. The craft seemed headed into a thicket of brush that glowed with the face of my mother (sho passed to spirit several years ago). As we hit the thicket, I snapped back into my physical body, quite startled. From the colors I was sure that this was my first astral experience, so I tried to decide its meaning. Suddenly I panicked! My sister was traveling by air on a vacation and I hadn't heard from her for several days, but thought she was en route to her home. At three o'clock in the morning, I began to frantically call the airlines to find out if there had been any crashes! Of course there were none, and my sister called me the next day to say she was back safely. In retrospect, it's a shame that I panicked instead of just enjoying my lovely visit to mother."

How to Handle Yourself on the Astral

Before you attempt to go out on the astral in full conscious control, it is a good idea to consider what may happen and how you will react. First you must understand that the slightest reaction of fear will pop you back into your physical body with a resounding jerk. But this also assures you that you will not get lost out in the astral space.

On your first astral trips you will find that you take along most of your normal physical habits and limitations, but this is only because your mind has not made the adjustment. The astral or emotional body has essentially no weight and can be propelled by the slightest thought, yet you will find yourself walking or swimming on the astral until you realize that it is not necessary. When I first learned to project, I had several weeks of propelling myself through the air above the palm trees by a sort of breast stroke. Then one night I realized that I had brought along my three dimensional method of thinking that the body requires a visible means of propulsion. After that, it was easy to travel just by *willing* myself to be there—and I traveled at the speed of thought.

Control of your astral body is as simple as controlling your emotions—in fact it is the same thing. Thus the work you have already done to build your constructive will can be easily applied to controlling your astral experiences. It is best to stay in and around your house for the first few trips. Then as you get the feel of it, extend your expeditions gradually to include the fascinating realms of the spirit world. With this brief discussion in mind, let's turn to a ritual to bring you out of your body in full consciousness.

Ritual to Take You Directly
Out of Your Body While Fully Conscious

The preparation and materials for this ritual are the same as for the Ritual to Program Your Subconscious Mind to Induce Astral Travel. Follow the first two steps of the ritual just as if it were for the subconscious programming ritual (See p. 188). We will pick up at step three.

Ritual Step #3: Anoint your brow with the astral travel oil, and chant:

> Wonderous spirits of the air,
>> This lovely fragrance let us share
> Upon the astral realms so fair.
>> Attend me now as I come there.
> Help loose the body's hold on me,
>> That I may soar up light and free.
> Now Light and Love I'll share with friends,
>> And knowledge gain that knows no ends.
> Hear this, my word addressed to thee,
>> And as my will, so mote it be!

Ritual Step #4: Again conclude the sitting up part of the ritual: "Now my thanks to all who are helping here. I invite my spirit teachers and loved ones to meet me as I float out onto your plane of life that I may share your happy company. To all elementals assembled here, attend me now as I leave my body, and when you are finished, return to your natural homes harming no one on the way. I come now into the pleasure of your presence. Blessed be."

Ritual Step #5: Lay your body comfortably on the bed or couch and focus your gaze on a spot in the air in front of your altar. *Will* yourself to stand in front of your altar as you chant:

> Now body, loose your hold on me,
> > It's good for you and safe, you see.
> I will my astral self to be
> > Beside my altar, light and free.
> I'm there right now, most easily.
> > And as my will, so mote it be!

Combine your chanting with the creative imagination that makes you feel lighter and lighter until you feel yourself floating out of your body, or suddenly realize that you are indeed standing at your altar without your physical body.

There is a critical point which should be examined here. The first time you try this ritual, you are somewhat unfamiliar with the chants and your subconscious is fearful of the new experience. Thus your first attempt may be quite sloppy and therefore produce no projection. If you allow yourself to become frustrated or discouraged, you will build up a block against success in the future. Use your constructive will first to get thoroughly familiar with the ritual, and then to win your ability to visit the astral at will. The "trick" is to keep feeling lighter and lighter as you chant—until you feel yourself free of the physical body.

A Student's Experience with Astral Travel Resulting in Better Grades

Larry S. was a high school student having a hard time with his history and geography courses. He just couldn't seem to get interested in such "boring" subjects, but he was fascinated at the prospect of astral projection. On Larry's third use of the ritual he found himself in front of his altar all right, but there appeared a distinguished looking gentleman standing beside him. Larry tried a friendly, "Hi! Are you my teacher?" To which the man replied, "I am your history and geography teacher for the moment." There followed an astral trip and lecture combination—Larry was taken to far away places and given a living look at his academic subject matter. Larry's grades in the two subjects quickly moved from D's to B's! But more important, he has a richer understanding of life and what it encompasses, and the feeling that he will now succeed in anything he seriously undertakes to accomplish through astral travel.

The practical applications of astral travel are as varied as your creative imagination. But it does require a high degree of discipline, and many people prefer to stay within the feeling of natural security of the physical body. For you desiring this security the technique of inducing prophetic dreams may be much more appealing.

Ritual to Include Prophetic Dreams

A classic of effective prophecy is given in the Old Testament story of Joseph's interpretation of Pharoah's dream (seven years of plenty followed by seven years of famine) which many credit for saving a great civilization from destruction by famine. But right *now*, in today's modern times I personally know well over a hundred people whose lives have been enriched by inducing and acting upon prophetic dreams. Yours can be, too! Let's start with the ritual, then follow up with suggestions for practical application.

Items for Ritual

Since we are not planning to go out of the physical body, a libation of prophetic dream-inducing wine will prove helpful. To a pint of your favorite dry red wine, add a teaspoon of the herb, mugwort. Let it soak in a consecrated dark place for three days, remove it, strain it, and chill it in your refrigerator. Put four to six ounces of the prophetic dream wine in your chalice and take it to your altar. Other supplies for the ritual include:

1) Prophetic dream oil (you can use your astral travel oil for this, or make a simple mixture of half citrus and half frankessence oils)

2) Astral travel incense

3) Your Lucky Meditation Stone (see Chapter 10 for details of consecration)

4) A small piece of scotch tape

5) A small piece of paper on which you have written a question or the general subject for your prophetic dream (for example:

stock market, job, love affairs, travel, would be broad general subjects. A specific question might be, "Will my baby be a boy or a girl"?

6) Your choice of white or green altar candles. The logical time for the ritual is just before your normal bed time. Be sure to put a pad and pencil close to the bed so you can make notes either first thing in the morning or upon awakening in the middle of the night.

Ritual Step #1: Sit at your altar and visualize the sphere of bright white light building up great power around you as you chant:

> Rama, Agni, send the Light to me.
>   Rama, Agni, send prophetic Light to me.
> Show me what the future holds,
>   That I may be strong and bold.
> Rama, Agni, send the Light that sets me free.

Ritual Step #2: Light your candles and incense and chant:

> Creatures of fire, I charge you now,
>   With lovely visions show me how
> The future may unfold for me.
>   What is ahead that I should see?
> My question asked on paper white,
>   Do answer for me this fine night.
> I'll face my future happily,
>   And as my will, so mote it be!

Ritual Step #3: Anoint your brow, throat and heart with prophetic dream oil, and chant:

> Sylphs and zephyrs of the air,
>   This lovely fragrance let us share.
> To set the mood of prophecy
>   And help you bring true dreams to me.
> Attend me in my dreams tonight,
>   And help me see the future right.
> That life may be a better thing,
>   And help to many I may bring.
> Your future knowledge share with me,
>   And as my will, so mote it be!

Ritual Step #4: Pick up your chalice of wine, toast your reflection in the altar mirror and all the spirits in the room. Take a long sip and chant:

> This cup of love we share tonight,
>   Then dream of ways to make life bright.
> Good spirits all, who work with me,
>   I thank you that you help me see
> Those things the future holds for me
>   And how to handle what I see.
> These words of friendship are for thee,
>   And as my will, so mote it be!

Continue toasting and chanting until the wine is about half consumed.

Ritual Step #5: Fold your written question into a small enough square to fit easily beneath your Lucky Meditation Stone. With a small piece of scotch tape, fasten the stone to your brow just above and between your eyes. Slip the paper between the stone and your brow, making sure that it will stay in place. Then address your reflection in the mirror as if it were your subconscious mind:

> "This stone and paper are your reminder of your assignment for the night. You are to bring me an accurate prophetic dream in answer to the question written on the paper behind the stone. When I awaken you will brighten my memory of the dream while I write it down so that it will be remembered and used. You know that this is for the good of our whole organism, and you must cooperate. So mote it be."

Ritual Step #6: Repeat Ritual Step #4 until the remaining wine is consumed.

Ritual Step #7: Conclude the sitting-up part of your ritual:

> My thanks to all spirits who have helped me here. Again I invite my spirit teachers to participate in bringing the accurate prophetic dream. To all elementals here, attend me in sleep, and when you are finished with your tasks, return to your natural homes, harming no one on the way. I go now to the ritual sleep. Thanks to all. Blessed be."

Ritual Step #8: Lay your body down and let it drift into sleep with the happy expectation of success. When you wake up, *regardless of the time,* make notes about your dream experiences. The only time to get it down is when you first wake up—it fades very rapidly after that.

How Unemployed Claude Found a Job

Claude S. had been out of a job for fourteen weeks and was nearing the point of desperation. He used the Ritual to Induce Prophetic Dreams with the words *new job* written on his piece of paper. During the night, he dreamed that he was reading the classified section of the morning paper. There was a circle around an ad for a salesman. Claude was a machinist and did not normally look at the salesman section of the classified, but next morning he found the ad he had dreamed about almost word for word. He hurried to apply for the job, and was accepted after a very short interview. He seemed to naturally understand all the hows and whys of the new situation, and is highly successful in his new career.

The Secret of Useful Prophetic Dreaming

This points up the secret of useful prophetic dreaming. There is always some action required from you after you receive the dream input. Claude might have shrugged off the dream as nonsense and kept looking for work in his old field. It is only the information that you *act upon* that can help you! Similarly, a dream of accident or tragedy should not send you into a frenzy of fear or grief. Take it as a challenge to the *action that avoids or eliminates the negative potential.*

How a Woman Saved Herself from Being in an Accident

Mary K. used the ritual with a general request—just the word "future" written on her piece of paper. Her dream was of an automobile accident. Her vehicle was hit broadside in the dream at the corner south of her house. She saw in her dream that it was the upcoming Sunday, and she was proved to be right. On that Sunday afternoon, there was an accident on the corner south of her house—one car was hit broadside. And as Mary Says: "If I hadn't paid attention and used the north road, that accident victim would be *me.*"

How S.Y. Used the Dream Ritual

S.Y. was concerned about his investment program for "no good reason." The timing was the late 1960's and the market had been doing very well, but S.Y. felt impelled to use the ritual to induce a prophetic dream, with the question, "How should I handle my investment program?" The dream was of gloom and doom, with the strong suggestion to sell all his common stocks and hold cash in savings accounts. S.Y. called his broker and ordered the sale of all his holdings—he cashed out for just over $550,000. In less than a month, there was a big slump in the stock market and S.Y. calculated that he had saved almost exactly $300,000. He later commented to me, "For two years now, my broker has been calling *me* on the phone asking for my feelings about the condition of the stock market. He thinks I'm some kind of a genius!"

CHAPTER POINTS TO REMEMBER

1) Out of the body, or "astral" travel is a fact. Learn to do it and you will find many practical applications for the ability.

2) Broadly there are two ways to enter the astral: 1) Use the ritual to wake you up while you are already out, or 2) Separate the consciousness from your body while you are fully awake.

3) Use the ritual to compel your subconscious mind and wake up on the astral as a method of getting comfortable with the idea. When you handle yourself well "out there," you will find it easier to go out while fully conscious.

4) Conscious control of your emotions by your constructive will is the secret of successful movement and accomplishment on the astral. If your early attempts seem fruitless, work on strengthening your constructive will before you try again.

5) Those who prefer to remain inside the physical body can find much power from the use of prophetic dreams. Use the Ritual to Induce Prophetic Dreams for answers to specific questions or a general glimpse at the future.

6) Any prophetic dream should be accepted as a challenge to *action*. To help it happen if you like, or prevent it if you don't like it. The only useful prophetic dream is one that you use as a spur to successful *action*.

Chapter Fifteen ✎

The Fine Points of Timing
and Trouble Shooting Your
Rituals and Spells for
Maximum Effectiveness

Since the days of the intrepid ancient Phoenician sailing vessels, our gallant men of the sea have taught us useful lessons. The timing of the seaman was and still is designed to take maximum advantage of currents and tides. Thus our ships sail on the outgoing tide and enter port with the flood tide. In order to predict the ebb and flow of the tides, scientific research discovered a correlation between the tides and the relative positions of the sun and moon. This was later proved to be the result of the gravitational pull of the two bodies upon earth's large masses of water. That energies from these and other heavenly bodies affect the lives of man and animals has been understood for centuries. Modern scientific studies of the various planetary energies and their effect on human life are masked behind terms like cosmo-biology or even astro-physics, but the plain fact is that they are studying astrology, and in the process slowly proving the statements of King Solomon from all those years ago.

Although it is doubtful that Solomon originated the Planetary Hours System, he certainly brought it to a peak of usefulness for the timing of magical rituals and spells. Solomon offers the student dominion over all the forces and powers of nature by proper timing of his ceremonies, but the student should take care to heed his command to use the powers only for good lest the higher intelligence that is guardian of all execute a just sentence against you. You may break the laws of man with impunity, but the higher laws, like all the laws of nature are self-enforcing. With this word to the wise, let's turn to the details of timing for effective Witchcraft.

How to Work with
the Tremendous Powers of the Sun and Moon

There is not a farmer in Iowa who would plant his corn in December. You will say, "Of course, that's winter!" But even our seasons are caused by the different amounts of energy reaching earth from the sun. In the same way as a farmer planting his crops, your long range, major projects should be started in the spring when the solar energies are increasing. Lesser projects may be accomplished with the push of the right tides of the lesser energies, but the really powerful building and planting work is logically best started in the spring.

However we certainly can't wait the better part of a year for our help, so we will consider the next most powerful energy—that of the moon. In addition to the moon's gravitational force, it is a major source of reflected energy from the sun. The power of this energy becomes very apparent when one tries to hide on a bright moonlit night. The moon's energy cycle begins with the tiny crescent of the new moon and grows in power to the full moon, then it slowly decreases to the tiny crescent to begin a new cycle. All projects of growth or building should begin while the power of the moon is increasing, and tearing down projects such as the breaking of negative spells and exorcism of entities belong to the moon's declining period.

Just as the sun passes through each sign of the zodiac once each year, so the moon makes the same passage during its roughly 28-day cycle. The zodiacal sign of the moon's position is almost as important to your ritual work as the condition of waxing or waning. A Farmer's Almanac or almost any good calendar will give you not only the dates and times of the new and full moon, but also the times and days that the moon enters each sign. The moon spends about 2 1/2 days in its travel through each sign by comparison to the sun's thirty days in the same relative movement, so we can get the moon's help much more often. For farming and thus for all growth and progress rituals, the position of the moon is considered fruitful, semi-fruitful, or barren depending on the sign:

MOON IN THE SIGN OF

Aries	barren	*Taurus*	semi-fruitful
Gemini	barren	*Cancer*	fruitful
Leo	barren	*Virgo*	barren
Libra	semi-fruitful	*Scorpio*	fruitful
Sagittarius	barren	*Capricorn*	semi-fruitful
Aquarius	barren	*Pisces*	fruitful

We should not think harshly of the barren signs, but learn to use them for the breaking of negative spells and conditions. And Gemini especially but also Virgo are the signs of communication and mental activity. Similarly, Aries is best for battle and warlike activities.

V.C. demonstrated the value of considering the moon in his timing in combination with the Complete Prosperity/Money Attracting Ritual. He worked his way through beauty school as a barber, and had no money for a shop when he graduated. Using the timing of the new moon in a fruitful sign, he advertised for a partner and made contact with a man who set him up in business. Again he timed his opening to be a new moon in a fruitful sign, and business was so good (with the help of the ritual and money drawing powder and washes) that he was able to buy out his partner in just three months. A month later he was ready to expand, and again the beginning was carefully timed to the new moon in a fruitful sign. Within three years V.C. built a chain of three shops—as a rough measure of the success from nothing at the start, we can tell you that he bought a house for $125,000 in the fourth year *and paid cash* for it! There are no obstacles to success when you combine good ritual work with the fine points of timing.

How to Use the Power of the Days and Hours of the Planets (Planetary Hours System)

There is a time during each day of the year when each type of ritual will have its maximum effectiveness. There may often be a situation where you feel that you must disregard the position of both sun and moon because you need the power of the ritual *now.* Thus we need a good working understanding of the planets and the days and hours which they rule. The seven major luminaries each have a day of the week named for them because they rule that day's activities. Let's seek our understanding of the days before we move on to the refinement of the hours.

PLANETARY RULERS OF THE DAYS OF THE WEEK

Sunday is ruled by its namesake, the Sun. The days and hours of the Sun are best for rituals and spells for power, riches, honor, glory, making friends, and gaining the favor of those in high places.

Monday is ruled by its luminary, the Moon. Moon-ruled days and hours are best for reconciliation, love, receptivity, female fertility, voyages and messages.

Tuesday is ruled by Mars. (The Germanic *Tiu* is Mars' counterpart, thus Tuesday is named for Mars.) Mars' days and hours are best for acquiring courage, military honors, overthrowing enemies, breaking negative spells and conditions, and all things relating to the martial or military arts.

Wednesday is ruled by Mercury. (Woden's winged house is the tie to the winged footed Mercury.) Mercury's days and hours are best for communication, intelligence, science, divination, writing and business transactions.

Thursday is ruled by Jupiter. (This correlation is to the Norse and Germanic, Thor, God of thunder, lightning and rain, and thus great power.) Jupiter's days and hours are best for obtaining honor, wealth, friendship, male fertility, health and opulence.

Friday is ruled by Venus. (Traced to the Germanic Mother Goddess, Frigg.) The days and hours of Venus are best for enhancing beauty, kindness, love, romance, happiness and travel.

Saturday is ruled by its namesake, Saturn. Saturn ruled days and hours are best for breaking negative spells, for psychic attack or defense, and for spirit communication.

THE PLANETARY HOURS

Many modern authors have looked at King Solomon's work too superficially and jumped to an erroneous conclusion. Thus you will find that the planetary hours as presented here differ from those in some of the popular current works on witchcraft, but a scholarly approach to the work of Solomon will prove the validity of the presentation in Table 15-1, The Planetary Hours.

Table 15-1: The Planetary Hours

Time (Ruler)	Hours from Sunrise	Sunday (Sun)	Monday (Moon)	Tuesday (Mars)	Wednesday (Mercury)	Thursday (Jupiter)	Friday (Venus)	Saturday (Saturn)
6AM	1	Sun	Moon	Mars	Mercury	Jupiter	Venus	Saturn
7	2	Venus	Saturn	Sun	Moon	Mars	Mercury	Jupiter
8	3	Mercury	Jupiter	Venus	Saturn	Sun	Moon	Mars
9	4	Moon	Mars	Mercury	Jupiter	Venus	Saturn	Sun
10	5	Saturn	Sun	Moon	Mars	Mercury	Jupiter	Venus
11	6	Jupiter	Venus	Saturn	Sun	Moon	Mars	Mercury
12	7	Mars	Mercury	Jupiter	Venus	Saturn	Sun	Moon
1PM	8	Sun	Moon	Mars	Mercury	Jupiter	Venus	Saturn
2	9	Venus	Saturn	Sun	Moon	Mars	Mercury	Jupiter
3	10	Mercury	Jupiter	Venus	Saturn	Sun	Moon	Mars
4	11	Moon	Mars	Mercury	Jupiter	Venus	Saturn	Sun
5	12	Saturn	Sun	Moon	Mars	Mercury	Jupiter	Venus
6	13	Jupiter	Venus	Saturn	Sun	Moon	Mars	Mercury
7	14	Mars	Mercury	Jupiter	Venus	Saturn	Sun	Moon
8	15	Sun	Moon	Mars	Mercury	Jupiter	Venus	Saturn
9	16	Venus	Saturn	Sun	Moon	Mars	Mercury	Jupiter
10	17	Mercury	Jupiter	Venus	Saturn	Sun	Moon	Mars
11	18	Moon	Mars	Mercury	Jupiter	Venus	Saturn	Sun
12	19	Saturn	Sun	Moon	Mars	Mercury	Jupiter	Venus
next day								
1AM	20	Jupiter	Venus	Saturn	Sun	Moon	Mars	Mercury
2	21	Mars	Mercury	Jupiter	Venus	Saturn	Sun	Moon
3	22	Sun	Moon	Mars	Mercury	Jupiter	Venus	Saturn
4	23	Venus	Saturn	Sun	Moon	Mars	Mercury	Jupiter

The luminary or planet begins its rule of its own day at the moment of sunrise, and also rules the first, 8th, 15th, and 22nd hours of its solar day. You will notice a constant pattern of hourly rulers never varying from the rotational order of Sun, Venus, Mercury, Moon, Saturn, Jupiter, Mars. Now what does it all mean to *you?*

Practical Application of the Planetary Hours System to Your Ritual Timing

It's easy to conjure up a picture of a "Casper Milquetoast," a frightened or uncertain type of person, who is afraid to go to the bathroom without first checking to see if the stars are right! But that is not our intent in this work. If all your ritual and spell-casting work produces the desired results already, then assume that you have a natural sense of timing that needs no planetary help and skip this chapter. But for trouble shooting of your rituals and planning for those most important ones, you will find the astrological background of Sun, Moon, and Planetary Hours tremendously valuable for predictable results.

I am still a practicing Certified Public Accountant and would like to draw from my business background for the analogy. Often a client will call me to ask, "Should I sell my XYZ stock at a loss for tax purposes?" My reaction *must* be to discuss the business considerations first. Then if it makes good business sense, we are ready to discuss the tax consequences. The business considerations properly understood may prevent us from trading a thousand dollar tax saving this year for a five thousand dollar capital gain next year. But if the business considerations are right, we examine the tax consequences of our alternative moves to get the maximum benefit from our planned action. Similarly, the pressures of *life* may dictate that we go against the tides of Sun and Moon, but if the other considerations allow it, we will add a measure of effectiveness to our work by picking the best day and time for our rituals.

How a Love Ritual Was Scheduled for Better Results

Marylin N. had been experimenting with love rituals haphazardly for several months, "with barely a nibble" for her trouble. When she asked for guidance it became clear that she had kept no Grimoire or diary, so there was no way to check the timing or content of her previous work. She decided to be more "scientific" about her work this time, and planned a series of three rituals. The first began at the hour of Venus on the Friday after the New Moon with the moon in a fruitful sign. Marylin chose the 7 to 8:00 p.m. period of Venus as the most convenient time for Friday and enjoyed an elaborate ceremony with the Complete Love Attracting Ritual. She followed up with identical rituals at the Venus hour (11-12:00 p.m.) on Saturday and the Venus hour (8-9:00 p.m.) on Sunday. There was a feeling of better power than before as she worked, and the next Monday at work three different eligible men asked her for dates. This proved to be the start of a happy social life that soon led to marriage and family. Marylin keeps a diary of dates and time of all her projects now in case she needs help for her rituals again.

How to Trouble-Shoot Your Rituals and Spells

In our opening chapter we suggested keeping a diary of your ritual work, both to have a record of your successes in case you need to duplicate them in the future and for trouble shooting your apparent duds. Now we can refine our suggestions for your record keeping to include not only the date and time of your ritual, but also the phase and sign of the Moon and the day and hour of the planetary influences. Obviously it is possible to calculate the moon phase, sign, and planetary hour at a later time, but if you made a mistake at the time you won't know it later unless you have recorded the influences you believed to be active. Thus the first step in trouble-shooting is to review the dates and times of the rituals and recalculate or verify the moon phase, moon sign, and planetary hour. Check to see if you took daylight saving time into account in the planetary influences—or for very special work, consider a slight variation of the basic system. Determine the exact time of sunrise and sunset in your locality. Divide that period into twelve equal parts (that may be more or less than an hour each—more in summer and less in winter) and treat the periods as the planetary hours. Similarly, the time from sunset to sunrise will divide into twelve equal parts to give the second twelve planetary hours.

If you are satisfied that your timing has been excellent, but the results you seek are not yet forthcoming, it's time to turn back to the Witch's Pyramid. If all four points of your pyramid base (constructive will, creative imagination, faith and secrecy) are working in balance, your *thoughtforms* created by ritual must grow up and manifest. Look to the four points of the base of your pyramid and rework the weak one.

How a Financial Situation Was Worked Out
with Better Ritual Timing

Clarence R. had been working for several months to improve his financial condition, but there seemed to be no result. In the trouble-shooting process, he decided that his timing was excellent, but in reviewing his use of the Witch's Pyramid, he came up quite lacking in creative imagination. He realized that he had no clear mental image of the financial gain. He renewed his ritual work but included an image of his paycheck bearing a $100 per month raise. Within a week he received a promotion on his job that brought with it a $100 per month increase in salary.

Determining Blocks to Success of Your Ritual

Somewhere in the timing or the Witch's Pyramid lies the block to the success of your stalled ritual, but there is one possible exception. As Solomon would have said, your guardian angel may see a pitfall ahead or have something much better planned for you. Thus the final step in trouble-shooting a ritual is using your favorite method of divination to ask if there is something better that you should be seeking. Myron D. had been unsuccessfully trouble-shooting his ritual for promotion on his job. When he tried the egg reading divination method to ask if there was an alternate approach, he saw a very clear symbol of one of his then employer's competitors. Myron decided to act on the advice. He wrote a letter to the president of the competitor, included a good selling resume, and held a ritual for favorable treatment of the letter. Result: Myron landed a new job two full rungs up the promotion ladder and became very good friends with the president of his new company.

If there is a way to summarize the techniques of trouble-shooting, it would be to review your whole grasp of the subject. Temporary failure must be caused by an obvious weakness in your ritual work or by overlooking the tool that would easily do the job. In computer programming, it may take as long to debug a given program as it did to plan and write it. The successful programmer doesn't give up or try to find a new computer—he methodically and logically works until all the bugs are uncovered and corrected. There could be no better advice to the ceremonial magician or Witch.

How a Major Executive Used
Ritual for a Big Promotion

T.W. was the very ambitious Executive Vice-President of a large industrial company. Feeling that he was stymied in further growth, he used a combination of the personal power and prosperity rituals. For three months, nothing seemed to happen and the basic trouble-shooting process had not seemed to turn up any flaws in his approach. So T.W. resorted to consulting the Atlantean Witch's Runes, with the question, "What is blocking my power/prosperity ritual." Only two runes fell anywhere close to the string. There in the immediate future was the Rune of Shiva followed immediately by the Rune of Laughter. T.W. decided to interpret the message as a suggestion of patience with the certain reward of success. He continued his ritual work with fresh enthusiasm, and in less than three weeks he was contacted by representatives of a firm considerably larger than his then employer with an offer of the position of President and Chief Executive. The salary increase was just over $50,000 per year with a generous stock option program and all the perquisites of the top spot, too. T.W. would advise the student Witch to remain enthusiastically persevering. Look what it did for him!

Quickie Rituals and Spells for Emergencies

The effective, well-developed practitioner of the ancient arts should find life quite free of crisis and emergency. When your protection, prosperity, love, and personal power rituals are working well, you seem to sail through life from success to success—until that old devil, *complacency* sets in and you forget the how and why of your charmed life. Whether from complacency or because you haven't yet developed the full power of your rituals, there may be those times when the world seems to blow up in your face. And when it does, there isn't time to run home to your altar—you need help *now!*

The power for a quickie ritual must come from work you have done at your altar in preparation for a time of need. Let's illustrate with the ritual to destroy your enemy's power to harm. In preparation for a time of need, practice a general form of the ritual for seven consecutive nights. On the piece of paper you use to light your special incense, write "all my enemies." Then use this modification of the chant as you light your incense:

> As this incense burns away,
>   All my enemies' power fades today.
> No longer causing me alarm,
>   Nevermore able me to harm.
> Immune to all forever me,
>   And as my will, so mote it be!

How to Handle an Attacker

Then when you are out somewhere and somebody starts "picking" on you, take just a moment to visualize your ritual. Mentally command, "This person's power fades, *now!*"... and enjoy watching the situation change to your favor.

Larry J. was at a cocktail party where an obviously drunk stranger suddenly took a dislike to him. The stranger launched a violently abusive personal attack. Larry visualized his "Destroy Enemy's Power to Harm Ritual" and under his breath firmly demanded, "This person's power fades, *now!*" The drunk suddenly looked confused. He walked to a vacant seat on a nearby couch, closed his eyes and went to sleep. Larry shrugged, and happily rejoined the party.

Defense Against Psychic Attack

Another good ritual to prepare in advance of need is the defense against psychic attack. Preparation for the power of defense is complete familiarity with the feeling of power and release generated by the Complete Ritual for Protection Against the Spells,

Hexes, Curses, and Psychic Attacks of Others. To have this one ready for emergencies, it is well to use the full ritual for seven consecutive nights. Take care also to memorize the last three lines of the candle uncrossing chant. Then at the first suggestion of psychic attack, image the power of the ritual, and chant mentally or under your breath:

> Salamanders, Zephyrs, true,
> Gnomes and Trolls, and Undines, too,
> Your mighty power works for me,
> Uncrossing as you set me free.
> Success and power NOW to me,
> And as my will, so mote it be!

Keep using the chant until you feel the power of the attack broken. Part of Tom C.'s job as assistant sales manager was the review and approval of the salesmen's expense vouchers. When an item on the expense voucher was exorbitant or not allowable by company policy, it was the custom to return the voucher to the salesman for correction and resubmission, but the actual practice was quite rare. When Jack, who was known as the company "magician," submitted a voucher for expenses of an unauthorized trip to a convention in a distant city, it became Tom's unpleasant duty to disapprove it. He took the voucher back to Jack, but his explanation fell on belligerent ears. Tom's only recourse was to say, "I'm sorry, Jack, but I have to act within company policy." Then as Tom returned to his desk, he felt a series of sharp pains around his head and a feeling of nausea. The words, "psychic attack" seemed to flash into Tom's mind, and he responded by visualizing his protection ritual. He sat at his desk silently using the uncrossing chant for almost ten minutes before he felt the attack dissipated. Within another fifteen minutes, Jack collapsed at his desk and was driven home in what the doctor called a state of nervous exhaustion. But Tom knows that Jack simply reaped the result of the negativity he sowed, and the ritual turned his negative spirits against him.

Any of our rituals can be used to build a reservoir of power for emergency use. As you practice each one, pull out the most significant part—the shorter the better—and store it away in your memory to be used when you need emergency help. Watch for the little signs of complacency and guard against that insidious way of weakening your defense. You can and should live a happy, "charmed" life. But it is true that the price is *eternal vigilance* ... use your protective rituals immediately when you are under fire.

CHAPTER POINTS TO REMEMBER

1) Bio-cosmic radiations (or just plain Astrology) have a definite effect on the timing of your rituals for maximum effectiveness. It will prove extremely useful to learn to go with the great energy tides instead of against them.

2) The sun and moon are the strongest energy sources and so require maximum attention. You may feel it necessary to go against the great tide of the sun, but if so, you need the lesser tides all the more on your side.

3) Use the period of the waxing (growing period) moon for planting and growth rituals, and the waning moon for defense and tearing down rituals. Of nearly equal importance is the fruitful or barren zodiacal sign of the moon's position during your rituals.

4) The days and hours of the planetary influences provide the short term push to help you successfully launch a powerful ritual or *thoughtform*. Attention to the planetary rulers in your timing of rituals will greatly improve your success factor.

5) The first principle of trouble-shooting your ritual work is to check the timing. How much sun, moon, and planetary hours power did you have going for you? Should you try again when the timing is better?

6) If the timing of your rituals has been excellent, but still there were no results, fall back to the fundamentals of your Witch's Pyramid and look for your weakness.

7) When your normal trouble shooting practices have not helped, use one or more of the divinatory arts to ask for the "something better" that you should be seeking. When a block is clearly from your spirit help, it must mean that there is something better being planned for you. Cooperate and win!

8) Be ready for all emergencies by advance preparation. Practice the key rituals and lift the triggering part of the ritual for

emergency use. Then when you sense a need, you can visualize the complete ritual momentarily, and bring it bear on *now* with the mental repetition of the key phrase or chant.

9) The price of a "charmed life" is practice and eternal vigilance, and using emergency rituals for sudden negative situations.

Chapter Sixteen

How to Enhance Your Powers
by Working Witchcraft
with Groups of People

S olomon's comments on ceremonial magic give a strong boost to the ideas of group power. His basic approach is that when a master of the Witchcraft arts wishes to produce a powerful or important result, it is well to have at least three companions for the ritual work. He further comments that if human companions are not available, the magician should have with him at least a faithful dog. But Solomon also stresses the careful choosing of one's companions, and their purification and binding by oath of secrecy and fidelity.

The Tremendous Potential and Power of Group Work

The basic principle of all group work is the amplification factor—that one plus one always equals something more than two! And it does, as long as the group works in harmonious agreement for a series of common goals. Regardless of its size, the group must have a firm and respected leader. Lack of firm leadership produces results similar in usefulness to the classic definition of an *elephant* as *a mouse that was designed by a committee.*

The soundest approach to group work is to begin in a very slow and deliberate manner, testing the power and mutual compatibility of each potential member. But the power to affect the "outside world" is great enough in the carefully built group to make the selection and building process well worthwhile.

In his book, *Wall St. and Witchcraft,* Max Gunther tells of visiting a group that uses its combined powers to influence short term fluctuations in the prices of individual stocks—with *profit* as the result. Other groups firmly believe that their ritual work has changed the outcome of various municipal, state, and federal elections. But most important from the individual standpoint, the group becomes a form of super-family that is quick to use its great powers to assist or defend a member in need.

The traditional term for a working group of Witches is *coven*. The root of this word is said to be the Latin, *coventus,* which means a gathering or assembly. But I prefer the idea of the English word, *covenant,* which implies an agreement, compact, or promise. Certainly the mutual promises are the foundation and stability of all group work. And there are rewards of love, prosperity, comfort, and security for each member. Wouldn't *you* feel better if you knew that a group of powerful ceremonial magicians had promised to look after you?

How to Begin the Organization of a Coven

The work should begin with just two people before you consider expanding to a larger group. The traditional number for a coven is thirteen, but it is better to take a few years to build an effective group than to have your hopes for an effective coven shattered by dissention and inharmony. The family is the logical place to begin—but only if there is true compatibility and mutuality of interest. Before beginning any ritual work together, solemn promises of secrecy and dedication to each other's well-being should be exchanged. Next, a simple *thoughtform* of love is built. Go to your altar together, light white candles and love/prosperity incense. First visualize the protective sphere of light enclosing both of you, then sit facing each other, but as close together as comfortable. Hold up your hands with palms facing the other person, and begin to direct the living force of love from your heart, throat, brow, solar plexus and hands. As your partner sends the same love energy to you, a field of power is built between you. The full power is built in ten to fifteen minutes of sharing the love energy and chanting:

> This bond of love and faith we build,
>   That ever shall our hearts be filled
> With joy each for the other's gain,
>   And each to soothe the other's pain.
> We pledge each our fidelity,

> And for our work, pure secrecy
> Attack on one, is on us all,
>   We pledge response to member's call.
> Regardless of what comes our way,
>   This pledge binds each because we say
> It is our will, accepted free,
>   And by this word, so mote it be!

When you feel the completion of the bond, you have created a lifetime committment. Even if you should immediately separate and never see each other again, the bond of secrecy and love will be there between you. For adding the third and perhaps fourth members to your group, the simple form of the ritual should serve as the initiation ceremony, but as your numbers increase, a greater amount of formality and ritual is necessary.

In the formative stages of your coven work, group practice of the basic rituals, with the chants modified to the plural pronouns (as we did in the work of Chapter 13) will add much power to your individual effort. Two can work together at an altar as comfortably as one, but when three or four are involved, the members should sit facing each other with the altar in the center. Thus you will dispense with the altar mirror for group ritual work, but the presence of other "living beings" adds much more power than your own reflection.

When to Admit New Members

When you find your group of four working well together, the addition of new members will become a serious step. Potential new members should be invited to meet the group *after* its regular ritual work is concluded. Each individual should be carefully questioned by the group to determine sincerity of purpose, dedication to the arts of Witchcraft, attitudes toward group nudity (if your group prefers its ritual work in this traditional costume), and if the person is motivated merely by thrill seeking or some ideas of a wild sex orgy. After the postulants have left the meeting, a secret ballot should be taken. The decision to accept a new member *must be unanimous!* Even then it is best to admit new members on a probationary basis, with the understanding that a second secret ballot will be held in 90 days, and if the initiate is rejected at that time, he or she is to accept the decision gracefully and bow out still recognizing the bond of love and secrecy built at the first initiation ceremony. We will suggest a more complete initiation ritual in our closing section on coven rituals.

Types of Coven Meetings

Regular coven meetings are called *Esbats*. Traditionally the esbats are held twice a month on the new moon and full moon, but this is often varied to suit the schedule and inclination of the individuals involved. The esbat is a working meeting with rituals conducted to build group power and further your coven projects. Here the character of a coven may vary from the materialistic minded that is virtually an occult investment club, through the greater balance of broad love/prosperity/growth/success oriented groups to hightly psychic/spiritual seeking covens. With most groups, the beginning period seems to be devoted to improving the material comfort of all, and then with the feeling of financial "elbow room," the deeper spiritual and psychic seeking naturally takes place.

Special coven meetings are traditionally held to celebrate the Grand Sabbats, and often the Sabbats as well. These meetings may or may not replace the esbat closest at hand. The Sabbats are the holidays and celebration days of Witchcraft, on these traditional days:

GRAND SABBATS		SABBATS	
Candlemas	February 2nd	Spring Equinox	March 20th
Beltane	May 1st	Midsummer	June 24th
Lammas	August 1st	Fall Equinox	Sept 23rd
Hallows	November 1st	Yule Tide	December 21st

While the esbats are the working meetings of Witchcraft, the Sabbats and Grand Sabbats are normally celebrations for enjoyment and renewal. This is the occasion for the feast or festive party after the ritual work has renewed the individual and group energy. We will suggest a Sabbat ritual in our closing section, but we leave party planning to your own ingenuity, imagination, and personal taste.

Coven Name and Equipment

It is the custom to name your coven after the ancient deity that seems most in keeping with the goals of your individual group. For instance, Jupiter for power and opulence, Athena for wisdom, or Venus for love and healing. Each individual would also choose a Witch Name in honor of the attributes you feel best qualified to express within the group. These are held in strict secrecy, and thus are known only to other members of your individual coven.

A coven symbol may also be adopted, depicting the power and strength of its ancient namesake. And some covens invent a secret handshake and password. Obviously, these are optional frills—after all, a maximum of thirteen people certainly should be able to recognize each other.

But your coven certainly needs its special set of altar materials. The leader's Witch's cord and Athame' may be used by him in coven work, but the other altar accessories should be held for coven work only. The Coven Grimoire is the repository of the history of the organization and a living testimony to its growing effectiveness. The altar with candle holders, incense burner, cups of earth and water, and candle snuffer can be of special value as symbols of love and group solidarity. The chalice should be large enough that all may partake of the communal cup without stopping a ceremony to refill it. The only special, "extra" items are four extra candle holders to use as the symbolic watchtowers for the meetings. The items should be acquired new and consecrated to the group work in an opening consecration ceremony. They should be kept always in a safe place, usually in the home of the leader.

During all ceremonies, the leader (regardless of sex) is addressed as Master (your Witch name). There may be other coven officers as the group desires, and the leadership of meetings may be rotated among the more proficient members of the group. When one who is not the regular leader is conducting a ritual, both that one and the leader should be addressed as Master. . . ._____.

COVEN RITUALS

Working Rituals (for the Esbat)

Any of the individual rituals given in the earlier chapters of this book may be adapted or combined to suit the needs of your coven—or you may develop your own rituals to more fully express the particular group personality. Since I have suggested a form of group adaptation of the prosperity ritual in Chapter 13, we will illustrate here with an adaptation of the ritual for protection against the spells, hexes, curses, and psychic attacks of others.

Materials for the ritual are the same as given for the individual ritual in Chapter 9. Only the nine foot circle will be used because a group of more than three or four would be too crowded within the seven foot limitation. The watchtower candles are placed just outside the nine foot circle at the compass points (east, north, west, south). When the group is all gathered and nude (or wearing coven robes if you have adopted them), the ritual is ready to begin.

Ritual Step #1: The members take places within the circle, alternating male and female as possible, and leaving the point on the east for the master. The master lights the watchtower candles, starting at the east, and proceeding to north, west, then south, and takes his place in the circle. To begin the building of the protective sphere of light, the master commands, "Let there be light," and as the group visualizes the sphere of light building throughout the circle, they chant together:

> Rama, Agni, send the Light to we.
>   Rama, Agni, send the powerful Light to we.
> Sweep away the things that harm,
>   Let them cause us no alarm.
> Rama, Agni, send the Light that sets us free.

Ritual Step #2: The master walks to the altar, lights the altar candles, and picks up his Athame. With a salute to the candles and the east, the master walks to the east edge of the nine foot circle and begins to draw the circle ritually, proceeding counter-clockwise as all join the Shiva Chant (exactly as presented in Chapter 9).

Ritual Step #3: The master returns to the altar and puts a spoonfull of salt into the chalice of water and stirs it well. All draw close and hold their hands, palms down over the chalice, directing the power into the water as they chant:

> Salt in water, by casting thee,
>   No spell no unknown purpose be,
> Except in full accord with we,
>   And as our will, so mote it be!

When the master feels that the mixture is well-charged, he picks up the chalice and as the chanting continues, proceeds to the east edge of the circle and sprinkles the inside, again proceeding in a counterclockwise direction all the way around the circle.

Ritual Step #4: The master returns to the altar, replaces the chalice, and lights the incense. All join in the Fire Elemental Invocation:

> Creatures of fire, this charge we give,
>> No evil in our presence live
> No phantom, spook, nor spell may stay
>> Around this place not night nor day.
> Hear our word addressed to thee,
>> And as our will, so mote it be!

Ritual Step #5: The master picks up the bottle of exorcism oil and returns to his place in the circle. He faces the person next to him in a counterclockwise direction and begins to anoint at least her brow, throat and heart (some covens will complete the process with solar plexus, genital area, and all of the body's orifices) with the oil, as the group chants:

> And now this oily essence fair,
>> Adds its great power to the air,
> Attracting spirits of the Light,
>> Protecting us both day and night.
> This charge is true and proper, see,
>> And as our will, so mote it be!

When anointing of the first person is complete, she takes the oil and begins to anoint the man next counterclockwise from her. The chanting continues with the anointing until the master is anointed by the last person.

Ritual Step #6: The master puts the lemon in the center of the altar and cuts it into four slices. He then puts a spoonful of salt on each lemon slice as all chant:

> All spells against us, congregate
>> You must go there, 'cause it's your fate.
> Bound to this lemon evermore,
>> Each spell against us, that's your store.
> All in the lemon now, we see,
>> And as our will, so mote it be!

All draw close and hold their hands, palms down over the lemon to direct the energy as they chant:

Uncrossed! Uncrossed! This salt for we,
    Breaks up attacking energy.
Within this sour lemon bound,
    Now kills all spells with salt and sound.
As lemon dries in salt and air,
    We're freed from harm and all despair.
Uncrossed and happy, now are we!
    And as our will, so mote it be!

Ritual Step #7: The master pours a dram of uncrossing oil into the top of the seven day candle and lights it. All join in the chant:

Fire and oil, now do your best,
    Uncross and free us with great zest.
Salamanders, zephyrs, true,
    Gnomes and Trolls, and Undines, too,
Your mighty power works for we,
    Uncrossing as you set us free.
Success and power now to we,
    And as our will, so mote it be!

Ritual Step #8: All sit down comfortably on the floor, enjoy a mood of peace, growth, safety, and mutual love as you chant together:

Spirit of the Great White Light,
    Burn away our psychic night.
Let us feel your loving care,
    Give us joy and love to share.
Make of us your willing tool,
    Let fulfillment be our rule.
That our growth may be a Light,
    Saving others from the night.

Ritual Step #9: The master invites direct spirit participation: "And now good spirits who are with us, we invite your direct communication as we sit expectantly in the silence." Then all remain in a relaxed receptive state, feeling free to share any psychic impressions or call attention to any spirit manifestations you may notice.

Ritual Step #10: When the master feels that the spirit communion period is complete, he closes the ritual: "We give our loving thanks to all spirits and elementals who have joined us here.

To the elementals, you are dismissed. Go about your appointed tasks, and when you are finished return to your native habitats, harming no one on the way. Again our thanks to all. Blessed be."

How a Profitable Stock Was Handled

It was April, the stock was selling in the 40's with management talk of taking it all the way to 100. During Step 9 of the Coven Ritual a voice seemed to speak to the small stockholder, saying, "Sell your S Stock." B.W. took heed—it wasn't such a bad idea, since he had bought his hundred shares at an average price of about twenty. He sold, then watched the big stock market break in May. The stock he sold for over forty dropped steadily to less than eight and stayed there for well over a year. He credits the voice he heard through witchcraft with saving him better than $3,200. That's a typical bit of happy fall-out from good ritual work.

Special Sabbat Ritual

Since the keynote of the Sabbat is renewal and celebration, I suggest an adaptation of a combination of the ritual for building personal power and the nature spirit invocation. Supplies in addition to the regular coven altar equipment are: (1) Power oil (see Chapter 9) (2) A cup of salt water (3) The large chalice filled with love potion wine (see Chapter 9) (4) Red altar candles (5) Psychic phenomena incense (see Chapter 3). The watchtower candles are set at the points of the compass as before, and the group members take their places within the circle.

Ritual Step #1: The master lights the watchtower candles moving counterclockwise from the east, then takes his place inside the circle on the east. He begins the ceremony with the command: "Let there be light," and the group visualizes the sphere of light building up to fill the circle as all chant:

> Rami, Agni, send the Light to we.
> > Rama, Agni, send the Light of power to we.
> Power to our auras give,
> > Bring through us the joy to live
> Rama, Agni, send the Light that sets us free.

Ritual Step #2: The master walks to the altar, lights the altar

candles, and picks up his Athamé. With a salute to the candles and
to the east, he walks to the east edge of the nine foot circle and
begins to draw it ritually, proceeding counter-clockwise as all join
in the Shiva chant (exactly as presented in Chapter 9).

Ritual Step #3: The master returns to the altar, replaces the
Athamé, and picks up the cup of salt water. With a salute to the
east, he walks to the east edge of the circle and begins to sprinkle
the salt water, moving in a counter-clockwise direction as all chant:

> Salt in water, by casting thee,
> No spell nor unknown purpose be,
> Except in full accord with we,
> And as our will, so mote it be!

Ritual Step #4: The master returns to the altar, replaces the
cup, and lights the incense. All join in the Fire Elemental
Invocation:

> Creatures of fire, this charge to thee
> A group of power we shall be.
> Our word of power, all shall bind.
> T'ward us all thoughts shall be most kind.
> Hear our word addressed to thee,
> And as our will, so mote it be!

Ritual Step #5: The master picks up the bottle of power oil and
returns to his place in the circle. He begins to anoint the person
next to him in a counterclockwise direction, anointing her brow,
throat, heart, solar plexus, genital area, and the body's orifices, as
the group chants:

> And now this oily essence fair
> Attracts great power from the air.
> Spirits of power, stay with we,
> A strong influence we shall be.
> This charge is true and proper, see,
> And as our will, so mote it be!

The anointing continues around the circle, with each anointing
the person next counter-clockwise until the master is anointed by
the last person.

Ritual Step #6: All raise their hands and hold them, palms
forward, to focus the energy at the center of the circle (this is

normally occupied by the altar). The *thoughtform* energy is directed from the brow, throat, heart, and hands of each member as all chant:

> Form of power, built by we,
> > Filled with vital energy,
> Expand and grow, that you may be
> > Bright enough for all to see.
> Extend our power far and wide,
> > Whome're you touch be on our side.
> Fame, acceptance, open doors,
> > We earn together, more and more.
> All creatures like to have us near,
> > Old enemies now call us dear.
> Success that's bright for all to see,
> > And as our will, so mote it be!

Ritual Step #7: All sit down comfortably on the floor, and enter a mood of joy and peace. The master picks up the chalice and leads the Nature Spirit Invocation, but all should join in the chant:

> Little people everywhere,
> > Your fun and love we seek to share.
> Gronkydoodles, hear our call,
> > Leprechauns, come one and all.
> Leader, Gob, of Gnome and Troll,
> > Come and share your humor, droll.
> Paralda, Zephyrs of the air,
> > Caress us while our skin is bare.
> Salamanders, led by Djin,
> > The candle flames you may play in.
> Nature spirits of all sort,
> > In friendship let us now cavort.
> Children of love for you we'll be,
> > Our mood is light as you can see.
> And always as you sing and play,
> > We feel our problems fade away.
> Your laughter, love and fun come through,
> > And help us feel alive like you.

After each completion of the chant, the master toasts the al with the chalice, takes a drink and passes it to the member next him (counterclockwise). Each toasts and drinks. When the cup returns to the master, he starts the chant again.

After three or more uses of the chant, the master invites direct spirit participation: "And now, good spirits who are with us, we invite your direct communication as we sit expectantly in the silence." All then remain in a relaxed, receptive state, feeling free to enter trance, share any psychic impressions, or call attention to any spirit manifestations you may notice."

Ritual Step #8: When the master feels that the spirit communion period is complete (at times he may have to act as panel moderator for spirits speaking through members if he is not in trance himself), he closes the ritual: "We give our loving thanks to all spirits and elementals who have joined us here. To the elementals, you are dismissed. Go about your appointed tasks, and when you are finished, return to your native habitats, harming no one on the way. Again our thanks to all. Blessed be!" The ritual work is now complete and the group adjourns to the party or feast prepared in advance. Whether or not clothes are worn at the feast is a matter of individual coven taste.

During the spirit communion portion of one such ritual, six different individuals entered the trance state and brought through much useful help and advice for the others. One member received a suggestion for handling a human relations problem that had been a source of great agitation within her family for many years. And as is so often the case with spirit advice, it happily worked! Thus peace and contentment was brought to a previously miserable family.

How to Allow Trance with Safety at an Esbat or Sabbat

When you are working with a group of well-developed ceremonial magicians, trance is both desirable and safe. As long as your leader is skilled in exorcism techniques, there could be no danger—and the psychic atmosphere of a good coven meeting is such that none but the highly evolved spirits can come close to you.

The trick is to notice when a spirit entity offers to think "inside your head." Allow the spirit's thought process to inform you of the general nature of the message to be delivered. If it is compatible with your nature, let the spirit's thoughts begin to be verbalized through your own vocal chords and mouth. Don't worry about whether it is you or the spirit speaking. As the contact improves, there will be less of you and more of the spirit involved in the process. Some people are controlled quite completely by the speaking spirit, or are even danced around the room, while others surrender just the speaking apparatus.

I personally resisted trance for a number of years. Then at a midnight seance one Halloween, the group literally teased me into lending my body to Prof. Reinhardt. Many who have subsequently worked with the Professor will attest to the help he has brought them, but the personal help and guidance for me are enough to convince me that it is all worthwhile. In the words of an old television commercial, "Try it, you'll like it."

New Member Initiation Ceremony

When your group of four or more has agreed upon the acceptability and desirability of an applicant for membership, a ritual of initiation should be conducted. The best method is to invite the postulant to a regular esbat, and include the initiation as part of the normal ritual. The postulant takes his (or her) place in the circle with the other members as directed by the master. The ritual of the evening begins as usual with the postulant participating. In the sample esbat ritual given in this chapter, the initiation ceremony would be inserted between Ritual Steps 7 & 8. We will call these Ritual Steps #7A, etc.

Ritual Step #7A: The master announces: "We have within our circle, *(postulant's name)*, who has asked to be admitted to membership in this coven, and received the approval of all members. *(postulant's name, or Witch name)*, do you still earnestly and sincerely desire membership, with all its duties and privileges?

The postulant answers aloud. In the rare event that the answer is no, the master cautions: "Know that you are forever bound to total secrecy about this group and all you have seen here, under penalty of the direst punishment. Now leave this place with our blessings and think of it no more." The postulant is then escorted from the premises (after being allowed to dress), and the ritual must begin again from Step #1.

Assuming a positive response from the postulant, the ritual continues with:

Ritual Step #7B: The master picks up the chalice of love potion wine from the altar, toasts the postulant, then drinks. He then hands the chalice to the postulant, saying, "Now share with us this cup of love." The postulant accepts the chalice, toasts the master, and drinks. The chalice is then passed to each member, counter-clockwise around the circle. Each toasts the postulant, drinks, then passes it to the next. When the chalice is returned to the master, all raise their hands with palms facing the center of the circle and chant:

> This bond of love and faith we build,
>   That ever shall our hearts be filled
> With joy each for the other's gain,
>   And each to soothe the other's pain.
> We pledge each our fidelity.
>   And for our work, pure secrecy.
> Attack on one is on us all,
>   We pledge response to member's call.
> Regardless of what comes our way,
>   This pledge binds each because we say,
> It is our will, accepted free,
>   And by this word, so mote it be!

After each completion of the chant, the chalice is passed again until three chants are completed.

Ritual Step #7C: The master greets the new member: "Well come, good friend, we now are one. Our hopes and dreams are entwined forevermore." The master then greets the new member with a kiss or handshake, and each member of the group in turn greets the new member with a kiss or handshake. Then all return to their places in the circle and the ritual continues with step #8.

Some covens are a bit more physical in their greeting to a new member, but that is purely a matter of group taste.

Invitation to Astral Coven Work

How do I find a coven? Particularly if you live in a sparsely populated area, you may feel that the foregoing discussion of coven work is interesting, but not useful because you have nobody to work with. It has always been so! But innovative Witches have ways around any problem. Part of our research program in Witchcraft at E.S.P. Laboratory in Los Angeles included the establishing of an astral coven with participation by coven members not just in the United States, but in England, Canada, Africa, and South America. Naturally the disciplines of Chapter 14 become especially important to this form of coven work, but it is exceptionally rewarding to many.

If *you* would like to participate in our Astral Coven, or simply share your comments and results from the work of this book, please write me: Al G. Manning, c/o E.S.P. Laboratory, 7559 Santa Monica Blvd., Los Angeles, California 90046.

Blessed be!

CHAPTER POINTS TO REMEMBER

1) The reason for group work is the amplification of the power you can generate. When minds unite in a common cause, one plus one always equals more than two.

2) The traditional name for a working group of Witches is *coven*. A normal coven includes not more than 13 members—more would become unwieldy, and would not fit into the ritual circle.

3) A firm and proficient leader is the keystone of a coven. Without firm leadership the group produces only chaos, not results.

4) The covenants of the coven are secrecy, fidelity, love, and mutual assistance. It is indeed a comfort to know that a group of powerful Witches has pledged to look after *your* best interests.

5) The first two, three or four Witches may form the binding group *thoughtform* together. Additional members should be added by initiation ceremony, only after unanimous acceptance by the group.

6) Regular working coven meetings are called *esbats*. The major Witch holidays are celebrated with a special ritual and feast or party. The sabbats or Witch holidays are given in the text under Types of Coven Meetings.

7) Mythological and astrological lore should be considered in choosing your coven name and the individual names. The coven should have its own symbol, and its own altar equipment, separate from those of any individual member.

8) The esbat, sabbat, and initiation rituals given here are samples. From them you will be able to adapt and create other

rituals to express the individual group personality and work for its goals.

9) You are invited to share your experiences and results with me, and inquire about joining the E.S.P. Laboratory Astral Coven. You may write to me at the address given at the end of the chapter text.

Blessed be!